JOHN GREIG'S
BOOK OF FOOTBALL

It's a goal! Rangers scoring against Falkirk at Ibrox

JOHN GREIG'S
BOOK OF FOOTBALL

PELHAM BOOKS

First published in Great Britain by

PELHAM BOOKS LTD.

26 Bloomsbury Street
London W.C.1

© *John Greig 1969*

7207   0011   6

Made and printed in Great Britain by
Fletcher & Son Ltd, Norwich

Contents

Introduction by Denis Law

Denis Law and John Greig after a morning's training with Scotland's team

Last year I introduced the first edition of the *George Best Annual*, which was an instant best seller. This year it is my pleasure to introduce the first edition of the *John Greig Annual*. Having read through the contents, I am sure that John's first edition will also be an instant success.

There is a wealth of information and stories relating to Scottish football and Scottish players, giving the Annual, as was intended, mainly a Scottish flavour. However, in addition, John has also made sure that there are stories from across the border and tales of trips abroad which add to the general interest.

John and I have been team mates in the Scottish side on many occasions, and this has given me the opportunity of getting to know him well. We all know that he gives a hundred per cent effort on the field and, what I feel is equally important, John continues with this same spirit off the field.

A fine example to all would-be Scottish footballers and to the youth of the country, I am proud to have him as a team mate and a good friend.

Here's wishing you continued success John, and may this be the first of many more exciting *John Greig Annuals*.

Denis Law

7

All the excitement of a Rangers v. Celtic match. This shot from Colin Stein almost beats John Fallon . . . but not quite!

Denis Law – The King of British Football

by John Greig

THE flamboyant image that Denis Law presents to the world on the field is almost the exact opposite of what he is like when he is not playing football.

I will never forget the first time I met him as a member of a Scottish team party before a game against England. That was five years ago at Hampden when we won 1–0 through an Alan Gilzean goal.

I was a new boy, relatively inexperienced. The one international appearance I had had before was playing for the Scottish League team against the English League. That is never quite the same as being in a full Scottish team. That day, when I reported with the rest of the party, I admit that I felt a little bit in awe of some of the more famous Scots' stars. I was O.K. as far as the home Scots were concerned. I knew them through playing with them or against them. But there was a special glamour hanging around say the late John White of Spurs and Denis, who wasn't too long back from Torino. I wondered how I would be received by them, how hard it was to be accepted by them. At that time, I think that I was a little bit scared about meeting them.

I didn't have to be. John White had the knack of making any player feel right at home, just as if you were sitting back in your own club dressing-rooms. And Denis, instead of being the star of the proceedings as he usually is on the field, was one of the quietest lads in the whole group of players. He is still the same way. When you join up with a Scottish party at the hotel headquarters before an international then you can bet your life that Denis will sit down and order a pot of tea.

That will be him until it's time to go training or whatever we have on the schedule. I have never known anyone drink as much tea as Denis does. When we're relaxing at these get-togethers some of us might be playing cards, some might be playing billiards or table tennis but Denis just sits with his pot of tea, always ready to talk about the game with anyone – from the most experienced players to the youngest and rawest international player in the party.

He has been that way all the time I have known him. And, because of this attitude, I feel that I owe Denis a certain debt of gratitude. When I was first made captain of Scotland in the last World Cup, by the then team boss Jock

9

Moment of joy! John Greig raises his arm after he had scored against Celtic from a penalty. January, 1969

The Law on duty for Scotland. Here he is seen heading Scotland's first goal against England at Hampden Park. April, 1966

Stein, manager of Celtic, neither Denis nor Jim Baxter, both previous Scottish captains, were available to play. Yet in the next game when I retained the captaincy both of them were ready to help me in every possible way. Never once did they jib at the fact that I was the captain, never once did they question anything that I said out there on the field.

They could have, I suppose. Many international players with their reputations might have. After all they had more big game experience than I had. They didn't look at it that way, however. To their credit they tried as hard as they could to make the job as easy as possible for me. I will always be grateful to them for that support . . . especially, I think to Denis.

It was a little bit different with Baxter because I knew him so much better. We played for Rangers together, so it was easier for him to accept the situation and work with me.

Again, Denis had worried me probably because he was always a player I had admired so very much. You see, before I met Denis or played with him I had made up my mind that this man was just about the perfect player. In my own mind I had placed him alongside John Charles as a top player who has almost everything a top player needs.

When you talk about other leading players in the world you are able to say that they are a bit one-footed, or, at least, they favour one foot more than the other. You can't say that about Denis Law. He is a completely two-footed

11

The Law off duty. Denis outside Manchester United's Old Trafford with his son Andrew

player: He has the ability to use either foot with equal power.

Again, you can say that one player is good on the ground but weak in the air. With Denis you watch him doing something particularly ally fast reflexes, the fastest I have seen in any footballer.

These reflexes have made him the great striker that he is. He can lurk around a penalty box then when the ball breaks towards him he

'You watch him doing something particularly brilliant on the deck at one moment . . .'
You can't stop that man! Denis Law shoots for goal in a Scotland v. Ireland international

brilliant on the deck one moment then climbing above the centre-half to head a goal the next.

Then above all else, to add to his talents, you have his speed off the mark and his fantastic-

can move so much faster to it than anyone else. It turns what would be fractional chances for any other forward into goals for Denis Law.

I know that Denis has been criticized when he is playing for Scotland and like most of the

12

Bingo! Denis Law in characteristic
stance, after scoring against England, the
'auld enemy'

players in the team I think the criticism has been unfair.

Very often Denis has been asked to play up-field as the main striker for Scotland and been told to stay upfield. Now, in theory, that can be O.K. Denis is deadly as a striker, though, to my mind, he has a lot more to offer to a team than simply that one side of his talents.

Sometimes, with Scotland, he has drifted deeper and then been blamed when we haven't done well. Yet all that Denis has done is to drop back a little bit to escape a player who might be marking him so tightly that his whole job is being nullified. This means he must lose his 'shadow' if he is going to be able to do a job for the team. This is what he has tried to do then found that the fans don't like it.

Sometimes, of course, Denis becomes the victim of the anti-Anglo feeling that sometimes blows up in Scotland before international games. The 'anti-Anglos' are the people who don't want the players who play in England to be considered. I've seen these people suggesting that Denis doesn't want to play for Scotland, which is utter nonsense. Denis Law plays his heart out for Scotland every time he is chosen . . . and he probably plays extra-hard when we come up against England.

Little Nobby Stiles, a team-mate of Denis at Old Trafford tells a story about this. Nobby's first game for England was in a game against Scotland at Wembley. He felt a bit nervous as the teams lined up in the tunnel before they went on the field. Now he had two club mates in the Scottish team, Pat Crerand and Denis. As the teams were going out Pat was joking away – as he always does. He was kidding Nobby about the number of Scots in the crowd. 'This is like a home game for us,' he quipped.

That helped calm Nobby's nerves a bit. Then before the game kicked off he spoke to Denis.

Says Nobby: 'Denis looked right through me. He didn't even recognize me. Once he had that blue jersey of Scotland on that was all he wanted to know about. Everything else was put out of his mind.'

That sums it up. Denis has his whole mind on Scotland, on the Scottish team, and what he can do to help us win the game. It's the right attitude to have. I know that some players can joke away before a match with their opponents, but Denis won't. And neither will Billy Bremner of Leeds United. Billy won't say a word to any pal he has in the opposing team until after the match is over.

He feels it would upset his approach to the game. It is the complete professional touch and I tell the story about Nobby Stiles here to let some of the people who complain about Denis in a Scotland jersey realize how the opposition look on him.

I know this, that I would never leave Denis out of any team that I was picking. And I know too, that when I am in a Scotland team and know that Denis is playing too, then I feel our chances have improved before a ball has been kicked.

I think that Denis has the personality and ability on the field to inspire any team. Certainly he is the player that every opposing team fears. They all know Denis. They all respect Denis and when Scotland leaves him out of a team the opposition are all a little bit relieved. . .

To me he is one of the greatest weapons we have . . . and one of the greatest footballers the world has produced.

But then, of course, I'm a Law fan . . .

No. 3 for Rangers . . . and there's nothing Kilmarnock's Andy King, Sandy McLaughlin and Jackie McGrory can do to stop this Willie Henderson shot

A cat's reaction! Only a super goalkeeper like Ronnie Simpson could have made this wonder save possible as Rangers' Orjan Persson drives for goal watched by Celtic centre-half Billy McNeill and right-back Tommy Gemmell

'*I automatically think of Jimmy Johnstone and a goal he scored against England at Hampden in April, 1966 . . . from a ridiculous angle hammered a tremendous shot past Gordon Banks*'

Bremner congratulates Johnstone (centre) *after scoring. On left is Greig, right-back for Scotland*

My Scottish Top Ten
by Alan Ball
(Everton and England)

THE one dominant thought in my head when I am playing football is to win. That is equally true whether I am playing for my club or my country.

I am just as determined whether I am playing in a home Cup-tie against a Fourth Division team or thousands of miles away against some formidable foreign international side.

But if you were to ask me if there is any team I particularly enjoy winning against I would answer Scotland.

The next question must be – why? And any Scotsman should be able to answer that for me . . . For the same reason that Scotland particularly like to beat England.

The same emotions make victory that much sweeter for Celtic against Rangers, Everton against Liverpool, Manchester United against Manchester City – and vice versa.

It's the 'derby' atmosphere. The desire to beat the enemy that's nearest and biggest. The enemy that is the greatest danger to your own reputation.

There is nothing wrong with this attitude. It's good for the game providing the rivalry is kept within limits.

So you see that I am not insulting Scotland when I say I enjoy winning against them. It is more of a compliment.

Yet my desire to win does not blind me to the ability of Scottish players. I have met some great ones and, believe it or not, regard others as personal friends.

John Greig, who asked me to contribute to this annual, has been an opponent of mine in international and inter-League games. I know that John is regarded as one of the top players in Scotland and I must take this opportunity to answer the inevitable question; he would be a darned good player in England too.

I have always been impressed by his willingness to work for every minute he is on the pitch. He has the two essential qualities for a 'back four' player. He reads the game well and is a hard, effective tackler.

Yet if, as an opponent, you are content to concede him these assets and leave it at that John will take advantage. For he is also a skilled enough player to overlap down the flank and create a lot of danger.

After kicking off with a Rangers player I know Scotland well enough to switch quickly to Celtic. I'll be all right there. John Hughes, Bertie Auld and I spent a holiday in Majorca together.

They were good company and are good players. John has exceptional ball control for a big man and is a strong, dangerous raider.

Because of his size he is obviously hard to

Scotland during Celtic's great run of success, but he is also well known in England from his Birmingham City days.

Bertie is as great a character off the field as he is on it and gave me many a laugh in Majorca. Yet he is a very serious footballer and an ideal midfield player.

'He has a wonderful left foot with which he can place the ball wherever and whenever he wants it.' Bertie Auld scoring for Celtic against Dunfermline some years ago

knock off the ball. His ability to control it makes him an even more difficult opponent.

John also hits a good ball and once gave me a demonstration of his heading ability that I could well have done without. It was at Hampden Park in February 1968 and John nodded the ball past Gordon Banks for Scotland's goal in the 1–1 draw with England.

Bertie Auld has become a famous name in

He has a wonderful left foot with which he can place the ball wherever and whenever he wants it.

I have often thought that Bertie Auld playing between two strong runners would create a lot of danger. His accurate passes to men who run intelligently and well put opposition defences in a lot of trouble.

I know he has a fiery temper but I don't

18

Jimmy Johnstone faces a challenge from Dundee United's Alex Reid

see that as a fault. I've got one myself.

While on the subject of Celtic I automatically think of Jimmy Johnstone and a goal he scored against England. We won 4–3 at Hampden in in April 1966 but little Jimmy must have gained some consolation as he scored twice.

One of his goals was fabulous. He beat Keith Newton, our left-back, on the inside, moved along the goal-line and from a ridiculous angle hammered a tremendous shot past Gordon Banks.

It was typical of the great individual goals Jimmy gets and illustrated his ability to make openings for himself with his clever close dribbling.

Denis Law scored Scotland's other goal that day which brings me to one of the most glamorous names to move across the border into England. From Huddersfield to Manchester City to Turin to Manchester United where he has won Cup and League honours, only to miss a European Cup final through injury.

That was a knee injury which caused Denis a lot of anxiety, but before he received it I rated him the most lethal finisher in the world. His reflexes were amazing, his heading ability unbelievable.

One thing that is consistent about Denis is his determination to fight, and I believe he fights that little bit harder against England.

He scored the first goal against us in a defeat which frankly stunned me.

It was the first time England were beaten after the World Cup victory. Scotland won 3–2 in April 1967 at Wembley where I for one thought England were unbeatable.

We were never really allowed to settle into our normal rhythm due to an early injury to our centre-half, Jackie Charlton. Yet all the Scottish players hit their form that day and they pushed the ball around those big Wembley spaces to tremendous effect.

I doubt if they would have been able to do it so well if England had been at full strength throughout the game. On the other hand I don't know if the result would have been changed either.

Scotland played very well that day and made Alan Ball a very miserable man.

Denis's big mate at Old Trafford is Pat Crerand, another good friend of mine.

Pat has had tremendous success in England, and deserves it. He is a player's player; very unselfish and a wonderful passer of the ball to a man on the run.

He has great control of the ball yet will work very hard for his team and must be a wonderful man to play alongside.

Pat is also a bad loser, which, for me, is a good fault.

Billy Bremner is another great midfield player, one of the best in the game.

The little Leeds player is one of the best supporters of an attack I have seen. He is very clever on the ball and accurate in his passing, and he uses these skills to tremendous effect when backing up his attack.

Yet he can also tackle and destroy, making him a great defensive player too.

When Billy hasn't got the ball he is still in the game, chasing and encouraging in the manner of the born captain. If you ever get involved in an argument about the ability of Billy Bremner you can quote Alan Ball as one of his greatest admirers.

I remember playing against Billy in an Under-23 international at Aberdeen in 1965 and Scotland had an inside-left playing who was a complete stranger to me. I had never heard of him, but he played so well that after the game I went out of my way to find out who he was.

He played for Dundee, his name was Charlie Cooke and he has since become one of the most colourful players in England with Chelsea.

Scotsmen will remember Charlie for his brilliant close dribbling, but since moving to England he has become an even better player. He is more of a team man and this, plus his remarkable ability, makes him one of the most dangerous forwards in the First Division.

21

Who else but centre-forward Colin Stein getting the goal that helped lift the blues a little at Ibrox. This was Stein's tenth goal since he joined Rangers. And it turned out to be a very important one, too

He is very quick over ten yards which gives him the time and space he needs to control the ball and make the best use of it.

Charlie has become something of a controversial character because he does not score the goals a player of his ability always threatens to get. But to see Charlie on the move, swerving, changing pace, dribbling and laying the ball off is to be tempted to forgive him almost anything. A fine player and a great entertainer.

When West Bromwich Albion beat Everton in the 1968 Cup Final one of their stars was Bobby Hope.

Bobby must be one of the hardest men in the game to mark because he lies so wide and deep. With the ability he has, he can afford to. He hits passes long and short, with either foot, with remarkable accuracy.

No matter where he is Bobby is dangerous. He crouches over the ball, looks out from under that dark hair, curls his foot – it doesn't matter which one – round the ball then catapults it to where it will cause most trouble.

Put two strong runners ahead of Bobby Hope and you have a winning combination. Because he plays so deep he doesn't score many goals but, believe me, he makes more than his share.

Joe Baker. Now there's a good player. Before anybody reminds me that he is English – I know. We played together for England against Spain and Joe scored one of our goals in a 2–0 win. But I always think of him as a Scot, and if you heard his accent you would too.

Joe has been around since he left Hibernian, but he is still one of the best players to come out of Scotland while I have been in the game.

Joe likes to play one-two's which gives him the chance to use his speed and control. He is a brave, dangerous centre-forward who is very clever at handling the close-marking defender.

Joe comes away from him very quickly, turns, then takes the defender on.

No doubt he will still have a lot of fans in Edinburgh and I thought they might like to know what an Englishman thinks of him.

I have played against Scotland at three levels of football – Under-23, inter-League and international. Sometimes I have won, sometimes drawn and sometimes lost.

I have just about broken even which, frankly, is not as good as I would have liked. But it could have been a lot worse.

Aberdeen 'keeper Bobby Clark makes a fine diving save watched by Dons defenders Jens Peterson (left) *and George Murray*

Transfer Fees

by John Greig

IT may seem a bit funny to some of you that I am ready to write here on big transfer fees when I have spent my whole soccer career with one club . . . The Rangers.

Yet when you get down to thinking about it there's nothing strange because these fees affect everyone in football. They affect every team in the Leagues, every player, every supporter.

To explain just what I mean let's take a look at the first £100,000 player in Scotland, our own centre-forward at Ibrox, Colin Stein, the scoring ace Manager Davie White bought from Hibs.

He affected the other teams in the League by helping to boost our gates at home and away from home, bringing in fans who wanted to take a look at a £100,000 star . . .

He affected the players by raising the performances of the players he was playing alongside and also very often the opposing players who grew in stature because they were being asked to mark the most expensive player in Scottish football . . .

And he affected the fans by the power that every personality player has over the men who turn up week after week at games. They de-mand personalities, players with a magical touch about them and place a huge fee on a man's head and he becomes that type of personality overnight. The game thrives on stars. The game thrives on glamour and big fees bring that glamour . . . which is exactly what the supporters want.

This has become the era of the big-money player, the high-priced stars, the men who draw the crowds everywhere they are playing.

Colin Stein did it when he joined us. Denis Law, Jimmy Greaves, Alan Ball, they do it with their teams. They are members of the £100,000 club, the élite whose names spell soccer magic around the world.

I don't think it makes any of the other players the least bit envious. I talk here as a one-club man and I was happy, for instance, when Colin Stein came to Ibrox because I thought he was just the kind of player we needed in our forward line. He could do the job we most needed done at that particular time . . .

He could score goals!

We weren't alone at Ibrox in having this worry. It's the worry that has invaded most of the top teams at one time or another over the past few seasons as more and more clubs rely on defence to protect their League positions. It's a worry that has helped destroy once-successful clubs, even though the rest of their game could match other clubs. So when Colin arrived I was delighted. I thought it was what the team needed . . .

I didn't realize at the time just how much it would mean to the fans, and, in turn, how much it could mean financially to the club!

To look at the whole business of transfer fees realistically, they can be a tremendous investment to a club. £100,000 spent on a player can make a side successful and success spells big money to the top clubs – and I rate Rangers as powerful as any club in Britain.

The money can be repaid many times over by increased gate receipts, by the glamour games against the world's great teams that your star or stars can help you get.

Again, take Rangers as an example. In our first season in the Fairs Cities Cup the club had paid out a then record Scottish fee of £60,000 for Alex Ferguson from Dunfermline. In the first round of the tournament we played an unknown East German team Dynamo Dresden and there were more than 50,000 fans at Ibrox, a record for the tournament's first round. We set up a second-round attendance record at Ibrox when the West Germans from Cologne played in front of close on 60,000 fans.

We had a third round bye, then met Leeds United in the quarter-final. It was a capacity gate at Ibrox, an 80,000 all-ticket sell out with record receipts of close on £50,000. Then add to that all that the second leg at Elland Road was televised by closed circuit back to Ibrox and 43,000 people paid to watch the match on giant screens set around the pitch.

That gives you some idea of how the £60,000 for Fergie was paid off . . . and I've only mentioned three European games!

These games against the crack Continental and English teams mean money for the club. Money that Rangers have invested in players . . .

24

If a top player can help a team to reach those tournaments his value is fantastic to any club, especially to the really big clubs, such as Rangers or our Scottish rivals Celtic. It all helps add excitement to the game, it means that the game is growing, developing all the time, instead of standing still. You get nowhere in any sport by keeping things as they are. If new ideas, bigger ideas, perhaps more expensive ideas, are allowed to flourish then the magic remains with the game.

This has happened more in England than it has in Scotland because there are more wealthy clubs in the South and more fans to cater for. I suppose it was because of this that so many people were surprised when Colin Stein decided to stay in Scotland with Rangers rather than join Everton. I wasn't. Nor were any of the other players at Ibrox, nor, I suppose were any of the lads at Celtic Park either.

You see we know the rewards for reaching the top of your profession with either of the Old Firm teams in Scotland are as great as you can get anywhere else. That's why some Scottish players would always rather stay in Scotland with either Rangers or Celtic. That, and the fact that you can stay in your own country.

As well as that we get more opportunity to play in European games than most of the leading English teams. The competition in the South for European places is much fiercer than we find it here in Scotland. Consequently the teams cannot be sure of a place each season in the three major tournaments, the European Cup, the Cup Winners Cup or the Fairs Cities Cup. While more often than not Rangers and Celtic are in Europe every year.

That may not sound important but, believe me, for players it is important. Europe, in a way, is a training ground. Going to play games on the Continent can be like going to school all over again. You come up against new ideas, come up against players whose skills are so different from your own. You find out which countries have different approaches from your

'. . . the high-priced stars, the men who draw the crowds everywhere they are playing. Colin Stein (right) did it when he joined us'

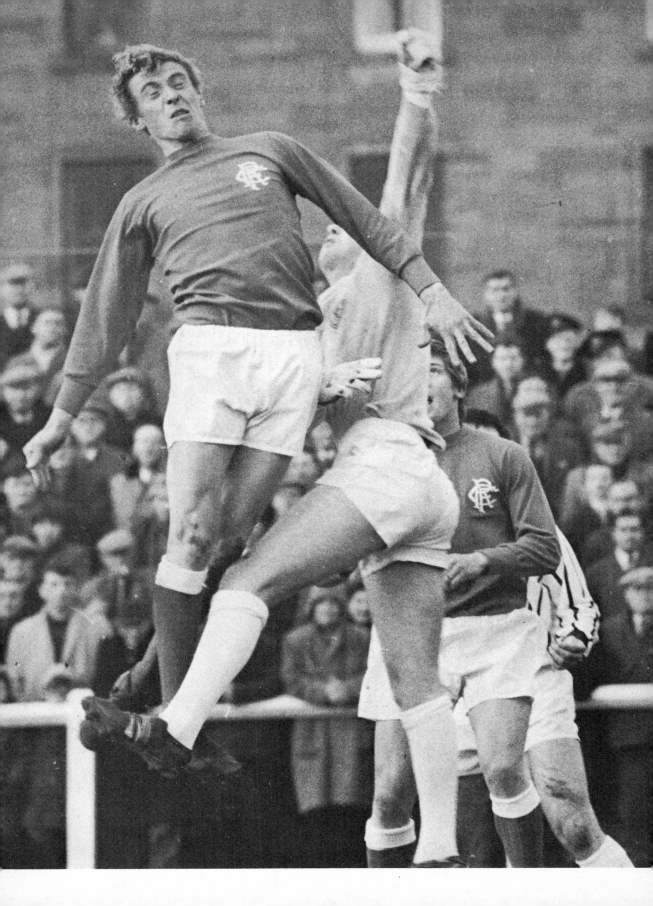

own approach, and how you have to alter your style to deal with their play. It is all so different, all so exciting.

In Europe I think you learn more about tactics than you do anywhere else. You get the chance to improve your game and the chance to heighten your professionalism. And as well as that you have drama and action for the fans.

When you have played in the Bernebeau Stadium in Madrid, or the Prater Stadium in Vienna or the jam-packed Rote Erde Stadium in Dortmund you are prepared for anything that football can demand of you.

And, if it means a club spending £100,000 or more to reach these tournaments then the money is being spent wisely . . .

Or, rather, it is being invested wisely . . .

An Old Firm match in progress. Rangers' goalkeeper Norrie Martin makes a flying leap to stop a Willie Wallace shot. John Hughes waits . . . just in case

27

Alan Ball 'a member of the £100,000 club'

Great Scots

by Denis Law

Last November, in the gloom of the late afternoon, the football supporters among the factory and office workers of Stockport had their day brightened immeasurably by the news in their local evening newspaper that Alex Young had signed for 'County', their local football club.

Only a few months earlier Young had left Everton for a short spell as player-manager of Glentoran in Northern Ireland. It did not work out and upon it being known that Alex was wanting to come back into English football the clubs queued to sign him.

Stockport County won the race, and on Young's first appearance in the blue and white colours of his new club – against Luton Town – the club had not only its biggest 'gate' so far that season but included among it were several thousand Everton fans who still idolized Alex, along with members of the production staff who a short time before had made a television film about 'The Golden Vision' as he was called.

The incident led to a few friends and I reflecting not only upon the impact the former Hearts' player had had upon English football, but also upon the tremendous part which has been played by Scots over the years, distant as well as near, upon the English soccer scene.

As an English sportswriter friend commented 'The Scots have brought glamour and skill, plus a lot of native shrewdness in administration to our game'. He said it, who are we to disagree?

Look at the soccer situation in England today from the managerial and administrative sphere alone. The Football Association, the premier organization of its kind in England, is chaired by Dr Andrew Stephens, chairman of Sheffield Wednesday – and a Scot.

Last year Manchester United followed Celtic's example and won the European Cup, though not the World Clubs' Championship. In previous seasons they have also impressed quite a bit. And, of course, not only is our manager, Sir Matt Busby, a Scot but we have one or two useful Scottish players in our side.

Last year also Leeds United took both the Fairs Cup and the English League Cup, and have been chasing the English League title for seasons. As skipper they have Billy Bremner and also have Scottish connexions in the

29

Alex Ferguson (Glasgow Rangers F.C.)

managerial sphere. Manager Don Revie's wife, Elsie, is not only a Scot but recognized down South as having as sound a knowledge of football as most managers.

Mention powerful Liverpool and you think upon discovery. Their manager? Scottish F.A. coach, Dave Russell.

Go back, way back, to the inception of the English League at a meeting in London on March 22, 1888, when Aston Villa, Blackburn

We dug into our photograph library to find this picture of Tommy Docherty in action during his playing days with Arsenal

immediately of Bill Shankly; when several top clubs became managerless last season who was top of the list of wanted men as a successor? Jimmy Scoular of Cardiff City.

When top Spanish club Atletico Bilbao wanted a British boss they approached Tommy Docherty; in the lower regions Tranmere Rovers caught the eye with young discovery

Rovers, Bolton Wanderers, Burnley, Derby County, Everton, Notts County, Preston North End, Stoke, West Bromwich Albion, and Wolves formed the set-up. Go back to that meeting and ask who convened it. William McGregor of Aston Villa. Another Scot, of course!

The list is by no means complete. Mention

30

Alex Young in action for Everton against Newcastle

Burnley's Harry Thomson makes a spectacular but unsuccessful effort to save this goal scored by Derek Dougan (Wolves)

also the names of such noted managers down South as Scot Symon and Andy Beattie at Preston, Matt (Jimmy) Gillies at Nottingham Forrest and you can think of so many more.

It's the same on the field itself. Around the middle of last season I ran through the players of note with the clubs in the top two Divisions of the English League. It was interesting, almost amazing, for its variety as well as its length.

Going in alphabetical order I thought of Arsenal's Frank McLintock; Burnley goalkeeper Harry Thomson; the Chelsea foursome of Eddie McCreadie, Jim Thomson, John Boyle and Charlie Cooke.

At Coventry there was Ian Gibson, at Ever-

ton 'Sandy' Brown, Leeds had Bremner and Eddie Gray, at Leicester there was Davie Gibson and Bob Roberts, Liverpool had that down the middle trio of Tommy Lawrence, Ron Yeats and Ian St John.

Manchester City had added Arthur Mann to the name of Bobby Kennedy; over at Old Trafford, in addition to Paddy Crerand and myself there was John Fitzpatrick, Jimmy Ryan and Frank Kopel; at Newcastle the names of John McNamee and Bob Moncur sprang to mind while at Forest there was another threesome in Jim Baxter, Bob McKinley and Dave Hilley.

Sheffield Wednesday could sport Jim McCalliog, Southampton Hugh Fisher, Sun-

32

derland had George Kinnell, Ian Porterfield, Ralph Brand, George Herd and George Mulhall.

Tottenham could show Jimmy Robertson and only just previously had seen Dave Mackay go to Derby County, while at West Ham Bobby Ferguson and John Cushley were outstanding. And Wolves had another Scottish goalkeeper in Evan Williams, born in Dumbarton.

At the time of thinking upon these players they were all playing a prominent part in their sides, and have you noticed something else? All those names were just from the First Division in England. There's not enough space to go through the full four sections!

Not that I believe there's anything unusual in all this, either in numbers or in quality. Scot-

land has been providing top players, of both skill and glamour, ever since Willie McGregor first called that meeting of clubs way back in 1888.

Here again, the list would be too long to enumerate. We'd need an annual on its own almost to do that, but let's stay with the thought awhile and pick out a few names at random – some of those who have journeyed down South to become idols of the English football fans.

Close to today one thinks immediately of the late John White, that 'Grey ghost' of Spurs, the boy who flitted so deceptively about the field but instituted so many of their successful ploys; of Bobby Johnstone's great contribution to Manchester City, performances which had the

Charlie Cooke (Scotland) beats Keith Newton (England) in an international at Hampden

fans of Maine Road wondering wistfully what their club would have achieved with the other four – Smith, Reilly, Turnbull and Ormond – of that 'Famous Five' of Hibs.

Nearer the border there was Bobby Mitchell with that magic wand of a left leg for Newcastle United; in Yorkshire, and, of course, earlier at Everton, there was that other Bobby, Collins. There was Jimmy Scoulars' great part as a player in Newcastle United's F.A. Cup records of the 1950s and Sir Matt Busby and Bill Shankly's part in the pre-war performances of Manchester City and Liverpool and Preston respectively. Not to mention 'the Doc' when he took over the white shirt of North End from Bill Shankly.

Further back still the names of other greats, indeed immortals, flit across the soccer scene. Bobby Ancell of Newcastle and Frank Brennan of the same club; goalkeeper Kenny Campbell of Liverpool, who played for Scotland with fellow Anfield 'keeper Elisha Scott in goal for Ireland at the other end of the park!

Preston, in addition to Andy Beattie, Shankly and Docherty, provided Willie Cunningham among others for the Scottish team. Alex Forbes was there as well in the late 1940s and early 1950s from first Sheffield United then Arsenal and some twenty years earlier there was another name for the dads if not the lads to dwell upon – the one and only Hughie Gallacher.

Still with me dads. There was another around that time too, wasn't there, by the name of Alex James, old 'Baggy pants' himself, showing North-End and Arsenal fans a thing or two – or three!

Later on came Billy Liddell, first on the wing, then coming back to even greater international glory at centre-forward. He's still taking time off from his post at Liverpool University to thrill crowds in charity games.

Also in Lancashire, at Maine Road, they still talk of Jimmy McMullan of the 1920s just as at Villa Park the older fan still chats nostalgically of Alex Massie.

At the risk of repeating myself I must stress that I have not mentioned all those who deserve to be, some may have slipped my mind or there is just not the space to list them all. I hope any omitted will forgive the fact.

But my main purpose in this article was not to present a list of Scots who have come South and stormed into the headlines of the Press and the hearts of the fans over the years. It was not my intention to present any such list but one cannot help doing so. There are, and have been so many.

Rather, when I started to write this piece, it was my intention to show that all the good in football has not been one way, a thought occasioned by a remark I heard recently about the Anglos in English soccer.

The point was made, around the time I believe, of that proposal to re-introduce a maximum wage in English football, that football had indeed done well for its players, and not only the English but the Scots, Welsh and Irish in the game down South.

The point was a fair one, the game has been good to us overall, but I couldn't help thinking that in turn the Scots have not done too badly by the English either!

It was then that I started to compile my mental list of the part, the glorious part, played by Scots in English football. And, having made a mental note, I felt it worth putting on paper. I hope you'll agree.

It's a Super Idea

by George Best

CELTIC for Highbury, Rangers to Old Trafford, Kilmarnock to White Hart Lane and Dundee United to Goodison Park. No sir, I've not taken leave of my senses, just indulging in a little soccer fantasy. The pity of it is that the trips down South for the Scottish clubs I've just mentioned look like remaining just that – a pleasant if unproductive pipe-dream.

For, as the astute ones among you will have surmised, I have in recent weeks been once again toying with the idea of a British Super League for soccer. And I'm not alone in entertaining such ideas.

I have a fairly wide circle of friends down South and over in Ireland. Although most are in football or fans of the game, quite a few are not. But there's one thing at least they all have in common. That's an interest in the major football clubs of Scotland.

Now and then, and not nearly on enough occasions, we in England see the visit of a Scottish club – as in the cases of Celtic to Liverpool and Rangers, etc. to Elland Road – in one of the European competitions; occasionally in friendly fixtures.

I have, whenever possible, taken time off from my footballing duties with Manchester United or my business interests in my two shops to attend these matches, along with my Old Trafford colleague Pat 'Paddy' Crerand, a fanatic who would, incidentally, stop his car in any street to watch a bunch of kids kicking a ball about.

In visiting these games I have been doing only what thousands of other English-based football fans have done, and after the games, in conversations about the match, one big point always emerges.

It is the terrific interest shown in the visits down South of the major Scottish sides, coupled with the wish that more could be seen of them south of the border in really competitive matches.

So far we have had to rely upon those European competitions I have already mentioned for this and for the present it looks as if we shall have to continue to do so. But why cannot we at some future date have a British Super League? And in the not too distant future at that.

I know that there would be plenty of oppo-

35

sition against this proposal. One has only to live in England a short-time to hear, by one way or another, of the quasi-official line about there either being a type of Super League already in England or the trouble which would be

There is, I suppose, a case to be made in this direction, but should this stop us giving realistic thought to a British Super League of the future? I trust not, the implications may be almost frightening from an administrative

Denis Law tries his famous scissors kick, watched by Bobby Charlton

created by the establishment of a new major League.

I suppose that if I venture to suggest that difficulties are made to be overcome I shall be told that it's easy to say such things as a player, but as an official one would appreciate the difficulties involved more, and possibly be a little more cautious about coming out in support of a Super League.

angle but they are also intriguing from a playing and spectator's viewpoint. Let's look at one or two of them.

Number one is the variety it would bring to the football of both countries. In English football today it is often said that even before a season starts you can take four sides and from them pick the champions and runners-up for the end of the season. I would say that if you

37

Colin Stein (Rangers) shows a glimpse of the opportunism that make him a £100,000 player as he beats Clyde's left-back

stretched that four to six that this suggestion would be about true.

The same, as you no doubt know better than me, goes in Scotland – only more so. Up there it seems to us 'foreigners' that you can name about three clubs at the most who will win almost everything before the season has even got under way.

Although this may be fine and dandy if you're an official, player, or fan of one of these top clubs, it can I suspect, be not only boring for the uncommitted populace of other clubs but at times a trifle boring even for those top ones.

Against this, think of the new interest which would be created if a Super League came into being and the fans in England could see Celtic, Rangers, Killie and others matched against the best in their country and you fans up there could see the best in England coming North to play regular competitive football.

My second point really follows on from the first in that it is the chance which would arise in such a set-up for the fans of football in both countries to see more of the best players from the other side of the border.

We in England are fortunate in that through the influx of top 'Anglos' into the Football League we can see the likes of Denis Law, Eddie McCreadie, Ian Ure, Billy Bremner and Alan Gilzean to mention but a few regularly, but we know there are many other fine players up there that we'd like to see in action but are at present unable to.

Certainly the annual Scotland–England international affords the fans down South the chance to see your capped players, but I'm not thinking of those alone. What about the others, the players either on the fringe or if not, still attracting the attention of the English fans?

Let me illustrate this with one particular case, that of Colin Stein of Rangers. When he rejected that move to Everton and went instead to Ibrox and immediately got among the goals last year the interest in Colin was fantastic south of the border. So much so that the Sun-

day newspapers invariably found room in the round-up of Saturday Soccer in England to bring in a mention on Colin – and others up your way were catching the eye.

Now if my Super League had been running then there would have been an opportunity for the fans down here to have seen the boy, and the many others you are no doubt keeping up your competent soccer sleeves.

The same applies in the other direction. If I know my Scottish football follower as well as I believe I do I am sure that they in turn would like the chance to see some of the non-Anglo stars of the English League in operation in Scotland.

The same can be said of some of the English sides. Take Everton and Alan Ball for example. Here you have a great combination, a club and a player who together could well prove within a short space of time to be one of the outstanding English club sides of the decade.

Across the park from them, literally, there is Liverpool, a club not only managed by a Scot in Bill Shankly but containing several outstanding players of both nationalities as well.

Leeds, Arsenal, ourselves at Old Trafford, all are sides I'm sure would add spice to the Scottish soccer scene in a Super-League set-up just as your Rangers, Celtic and the others would do the same for the English view.

My third point is one which has seen fans on both sides of the border arguing for years, I mean of course the respective merits of Scottish and English football. I suppose that according to one's nationality so is one influenced. But if this is so I suppose that as an Irishman I can claim to be neutral, well, almost so.

Seriously though, we do hear a great deal about how Scottish clubs would fare against English sides, and vice versa. And I don't think you can take the odd result – and you can read that word 'odd' whichever way you wish – as a true example.

I remember when we at United came up to play Celtic in a pre-season game and were beaten – 4–1 I think. That night we had plenty of folk around Glasgow, well half of it at least, letting us know that this proved that Scottish football was better than that in England.

Yet not only did we soon after go on a tour of Germany and Austria which saw us suffering several defeats but later went on to win the European Cup.

But when Liverpool beat Celtic in the European Cup Winners' Cup it was said in some sections of English soccer, and no prizes for guessing which areas, that this proved that English football was better than its Scottish counterpart.

I would, in all seriousness, suggest that neither attitude was right, neither assumption correct. If one is ever to settle any argument on such matters then any worthwhile conclusion could be arrived at only in a series of encounters, such as provided by a Super League.

But despite all the above arguments I feel that one of the greatest in favour of a new set-up in our soccer within the British Isles is the decreasing time it takes to get from one spot on the globe to another, and the ever increasing interest by one country's football fans in the game as played beyond their shores, let alone over the border.

I remember a sportswriter friend of mine returning from an England tour which included a visit behind the Iron Curtain. Impressing him most was the knowledge displayed by the residents over there of our British teams and players.

As he put it to me 'If they had known only of the top clubs and their players that would have been interesting, but they displayed quite fascinating knowledge of clubs in the lower regions and the players in those clubs'.

Although we players do not perhaps meet the overseas fans as much as do the Press when on tour I can vouch for the same knowledge shown by most of those I have met. For how long can this thirst for more information and genuine interest in the game in other countries be contained within the present European competitions?

One could not be far wrong in assuming that eventually, and perhaps sooner than later, we shall indeed have a European League of sorts. Of course it may be a few seasons away, but if there is a straw in the wind in this direction should we not recognize the narrowing of borders between country and country, between football fan and football fan?

If we do then it is not a long step surely to see that the formation of a British Super League is a natural sequence in the advancement of the game.

When it comes, and I think that is more likely than to say 'if it comes', not only will it be for the good of the game as a whole but it will also end many of the present-day arguments on the differing standards of soccer between country and country.

And don't worry if you feel that will mean there's nothing left in football to argue about. For there always has been and, I suspect, always will be.

Leeds arrive back with the Fairs Cup. September, 1968. Billy Bremner waits customs clearance at Manchester Airport

How We Relax

by Billy Bremner

EYES down for a full house. And the first number is – all the fours, Diana Dors. Number ten – Wilson's den.

Now these words, I know, will be familiar to many football fans who like their game of bingo. And they are very familiar phrases, too, to all the Leeds United players for whether they are at home in a League match at Elland Road, stopping the week-end in a fine hotel in London for a game with Chelsea or playing in a competition in Europe, the boys play a lot of bingo as a form of relaxation before their big games.

A lot of folk ask me how we spend the time before a match and they seem really surprised when I tell them that one of the secrets of our serenity before the kick-off is a house or two at bingo.

Norman Hunter and Rod Belfitt usually start the calling and then the winner of the first house takes over for a game and the winner of the next house takes over and so on. We usually put a little in the kitty to start with and that covers anything up to fifteen or sixteen houses . . . and bingo really is 'top of the shop' among the activities which help to relax us before the

time comes for us to run out on to the pitch and get on with the game.

When we are playing at home on a Saturday afternoon I like to have a big breakfast. Even when we have a game at Elland Road we often stay at a hotel overnight and both Jackie Charlton and myself have breakfast in bed. I always share a room with him and we start the day with fruit juice, a mixed grill and a pot of tea. Even if we've been staying at our own homes overnight, we meet at a hotel about quarter past eleven in the morning and most of the boys have a steak shortly afterwards but, for Jackie and myself, it's just a cup of tea. Then comes that game of bingo and then we go down to the ground about half-past one. I relax by watching television – either Grandstand or the World of Sport – and I always have a bath before the game. I find that very relaxing. Then, into the dressing-room about two o'clock and start getting ready for the match.

I like to relax on a Saturday night . . . and that presents no problems. I just go to the 'local' and have a pint of beer.

The routine for relaxation varies a little when

'Yippee!' cries Leeds United skipper Billy Bremner after he had hammered in their third goal against Standard Liege with only two minutes to go

we go to London for a game. We train Friday morning and set off to London by train in the afternoon. We go straight to our hotel, have a meal and then the boss, Mr Revie, always has a room booked for us for the evening. Here again we play a house or two at bingo and we also have a lot of fun at carpet bowls. We have one or two good players in the team, but Gary Sprake and Mick Bates just seem that bit more useful at the game than most of us. At one time, it used to be the routine to go to the pictures but times have changed and the majority of the team stop in the hotel all night and they're in bed by about ten o'clock.

On the Saturday morning, Jackie Charlton and I have breakfast in bed – just as we do at home matches – and about eleven o'clock the team go for a little stroll and they come back to

the hotel for steaks. But, once again, it's 'just a cup of tea' for both of us.

When we're playing in Europe, we usually fly to our destination the day before the match. That means we've often twenty-four hours or so to spend there – say in Italy, or Spain, or Yugoslavia – and it is at times like these that football teams have to be very careful about eating. For it's different food in different countries and what might suit one nationality doesn't necessarily suit another. I've seen Spanish people tucking into piles of paella – that's one of their national dishes which includes rice, garlic, squid and various other fish among its ingredients – with the relish that Leeds folk eat their Yorkshire pudding on a Sunday. But the boys play it safe by and large and we've been lucky with the food in most of

43

Billy Bremner pictured at home with his son Billy and daughter Donna

the countries we've been to. We haven't been very adventurous – but we've enjoyed our steak and chicken! After that we have a quiet night – a bit of bingo and a game or two of cards, perhaps.

Then comes the day of the big match . . . and there's no particular rush to get up in the morning. Normally we get up about ten o'clock and go down to the stadium where we are due to play that night and train there for about an hour. Then we go into the normal routine for a night match which is to have an ordinary meal before we go to bed in the after-noon. We are called at about half-past four and tea and toast are brought into our bedrooms . . . and another match is just round the corner.

So, as you can see, eating and relaxing play an important part in the pre-match routine of any professional footballer . . . and often when I'm at home during the week I eat and relax like every true Scot is supposed to do – with my bowl of porridge! I like it very much, but I must confess I don't eat it with salt like a true Scot should. I sprinkle mine with sugar. The people who spray their porridge with salt are braver than I am!

Aberdeen 'keeper McGarr dives at the feet of Marshall (Airdrie) to save

Mud in my eye! And the man taking a nosedive into it is Clyde goalkeeper John Wright in a match against Dundee. In the end the score sheet was blank

He flies through the air with the greatest of ease. Morton goalkeeper Russell saves brilliantly, with Ferguson (Rangers) in close attention

Her Majesty the Queen with the England team at the start of the 1966 World Cup at Wembley

'Excuse my foot!' Seeler of Germany nearly loses his teeth during the World Cup match against Russia

The Other Side of the World Cup

by John Greig

THINK of the World Cup, that glittering Jules Rimet Trophy and your mind conjures up scenes of Wembley or Hampden, or the Bernebeau Stadium in Madrid or any of the world's great grounds.

It brings back memories of the game's great players, the men of England, Bobby Moore and Bobby Charlton, the great Germans, Uwe Seeler and Karl Schnellinger, the Argentinians Rattin or Perfumo or the fabulous Brazilians, Pele and Garrincha.

These are the magical places and names of the greatest tournament of them all. These are the memories of greatness and glory and all the pageantry of this wonderful game of football.

Yet there is another side to the struggle for that golden trophy. Just as the big European games or the glamorous Cup clashes overshadow the bread and butter games played week after week during the season, so the grand occasions of the World Cup can hide the shabby side – the side that I experienced for the first time last season.

In the last World Cup game of 1966 for Scotland, when we failed to qualify for the finals in England, the occasion had been huge. We lost to Italy in the frenzied atmosphere of the Sao Paulo Stadium in Naples with 80,000 fans watching.

This time our first away game was so, so different . . .

We were drawn in the same section as our old rivals Austria, beaten 1966 finalists West Germany and the unknowns from the little Mediterranean island of Cyprus.

It was there on the sun-baked little island that we found the worst World Cup conditions of all. I don't think anyone would argue with me about that. The Scottish newspapermen who were with the team on the trip christened the bare strip of ground 'the worst football pitch in the world . . .'

After we had seen the pitch for ourselves and trained on it we didn't give them any arguments!

We had been warned about the pitch because Dunfermline had been to Nicosia to play a European Cup-Winners Cup game against the Cypriot Cup-holders, Apoel. After winning 9–1 at home at East End Park they went to play on this Cyprus pitch and could only manage a 2–0 victory. The pitch made that much difference . . . not any miraculous improvement in

47

form by their opponents. That in itself was a warning to all of us in the Scots' party.

If we needed any further warning it came in a most dramatic way. Just two weeks before we were due to fly out to Nicosia from Glasgow the international team manager, Bobby Brown jetted out to watch West Germany, our main rivals, play their game there. Previously the West Germans had beaten the Austrians decisively at the Prater Stadium in Vienna. This was going to be a complete walk-over for them . . . only it didn't turn out that way at all.

With the problems of the pitch coupled to a defensive set-up used by the Cypriots the full might of West Germany could only scrape a 1–0 win and that goal came in injury time. It was actually two minutes over the regulation ninety when they forced the ball into the net.

Any worries that Bobby Brown might have had about taking the opposition lightly disappeared with that result. He didn't need to stress that the game could be difficult. We had learned ourselves from that result. In a way, looking back, it probably helped us tremendously. It brought home to us just how hard this game could become if we weren't very careful.

We knew that we could not go there and take the Cypriots lightly. We couldn't take the slightest chance of dropping a point no matter what the ground conditions were going to be like.

And we knew, too, that these were going to be bad. Bobby Brown was so concerned by them that he decided to leave Denis Law out of the pool of players because of the risk of further damage from the pitch to his already troublesome knee injury.

We didn't stay in Nicosia, preferring the quiet of Famagusta. Originally, the intention was to train there but at the last moment the Boss decided that this was one pitch that we would have to see for ourselves.

I don't think any of us – though we knew it was going to be bad – had realized just HOW bad it would turn out. We expected some grass, at least. We were disappointed.

All we found was a piece of ground which resembled baked mud or even some kind of concrete mixture, with little stone chips scattered all over its surface. It was unbelievable to get this after playing on pitches like the one at Wembley!

We got down to training and found out the problems very quickly. The ball was bouncing all over the place, there was little or no grip at times for our boots. We tried out different types of boots and eventually most of us elected to use the ordinary leather boots with rubber studs which gave us the best feel of the ground.

The goalkeepers, Jim Herriot of Birmingham City and Bobby Clark of Aberdeen, had even more problems than the outfield players. They had to learn how to deal with the tricks the ball got up to as it shot off the stones – and they also had to try to combat the cruel cuts the same stones could give their legs when they dived in the goalmouths. They experimented with knee pads during training, but eventually Jim Herriot decided that he would play without them. That, believe me, took some guts.

Besides the problems presented by the surface of the pitch, the situation of the slightly ramshackle stadium was against the 'keepers too. The game was being played in the afternoon and a low sun sent its rays slanting viciously into the goal area. It was the worst sun I'd ever seen . . . but it did give me a bit of a laugh.

Just before the game began, at the shooting-in, I suddenly saw that Jim Herriot looked as if someone had given him a couple of black eyes. It looked as if he had a real pair of shiners. Then when I took a second look I found that Jim had rubbed dirt from the pitch underneath each eye. He explained that this helped to beat the rays of the sun. He has found after experimenting that this dirt rubbed below his eyes is much more effective than an eye shade or a cap. He uses it to beat the sun and also to cut the dazzle from lights during the floodlight games.

Anyhow, these were the problems and they didn't help us look forward to the game any

Pele – a picture taken during the match against Scotland in 1966

more. Then something happened to help us a little . . . the rains came. It didn't make the pitch so very much better, but it did stop the ball bouncing too badly and our strength helped us plough through the surface which had turned to sticky wet cement. You could feel it dragging your feet back every time you took a step.

The dressing-rooms were so bad that we had to strip in the Ledra Palace Hotel in Nicosia about a mile from the ground.

This was no trouble going to the game – but coming back was different again. By this time of course, we were in high spirits. We had won 5–0, two goals from Alan Gilzean, one from Bobby Murdoch, one from Colin Stein and another an own-goal.

So, though we were soaked through after the teeming rain which had fallen in spells during the game, we weren't letting it get us down when the journey back to the hotel started.

Unfortunately, the traffic was so heavy that the bus was held up and some of us – myself, Billy Bremner, Doug Fraser, Eddie McCreadie and Billy McNeill – jumped out of the bus and ran back to the hotel. The bus caught us up, but Billy and I finished the journey running.

It was hard then, running along a street in Cyprus, among the fans with our jerseys soaked and water dripping from our hair, to believe that this was the World Cup.

The other side of the great tournament . . .

Down goes centre Sandy Jardine . . . but the ball is on the way to the back of the net for Rangers' first goal against Partick Thistle

European Take-Over
by Pat Crerand

ARE we about to see a complete take-over in Europe by British clubs? I believe so. Regardless of what happened this summer, I am convinced that British soccer is about to dominate the world scene just as it did before the Continentals and South Americans matured in the fifties.

I do not say this – much as I would like to be able – simply because Manchester United followed Celtic by winning the European Cup, or because of Leeds United's success in the Fairs Cup. As a Scot, it is, in fact, hard to admit: but my reasoning is a result of England's World Cup triumph.

This made our players realize that the rest of the world's footballers were mortals, not gods. They were not so great, not so indestructible as we had been led to believe.

British footballers are physically braver and mentally stronger; they do not accept defeat as easily as Continental teams.

Which is why I say that, while we may not always win everything in sight, it is English teams that are always going to be the ones to be beaten before someone else wins.

If England's victory over West Germany at Wembley in 1966 was the first breakthrough, Celtic – my second love, next to Manchester United – certainly added to it. Their 1967 European Cup triumph over the ultra-defensive Inter-Milan in Lisbon was a tremendous thing for football. Even allowing for my partisanship, I know I was overjoyed.

The news reached me in the hotel room in Auckland. Manchester United were on tour and my room-mate Alex Stepney and I were listening anxiously to the radio before breakfast for the result.

As it came over, I whooped for joy. All I can remember after that is Alex saying, 'Don't worry, Pat, we'll win it next year.'

I don't know now whether he was joking, or really meant it. But his statement seemed so emphatic at that moment that it stuck with me. And, in fact, it became an obsession, not only with me, but with the whole team.

It was an obsession that cost us the League. When people say 'Manchester City won the title' it makes me boil. They didn't – we lost it because of our obsession over the European Cup.

At one stage in the League race, we seemed

51

to have it sewn up. I remember Jim Mossop writing in the *Sunday Express* weeks and weeks before the final Saturday that 'United had it won'. So we did – then we tossed it away, which meant we HAD to win the European Cup. For to players who have once taken part in it, there is nothing quite like European competi-

brick-hard pitch in Malta, with the fierce sun beating down on our necks; the cold, clear air of the mountains in Sarajevo; the six inches of snow in Poland; Madrid with its blue sky and Wembley with its beautiful green turf and the masses of people all cheering us.

It probably sounds hackneyed and old hat,

Pat Crerand (Manchester United) and Tommy Baldwin (Chelsea, 8) in an all-action moment at London's Stamford Bridge

tion. And as far as I am concerned, you can have the Cup-Winners Cup and the Fairs Cup . . . but it is the Champions Cup that carries the prestige.

I can still remember just about every tiny incident on and off the field of our European Cup journeys, but the most striking thing about our 1968 triumph was the contrasting climates and conditions under which we played . . . the

but the team spirit we built up during that campaign was just great. I know it should be there all the time but somehow it seemed even more so.

Gornik were the best team we played. And the conditions when we played out there were the worst we endured. The game should not have been played. 'The Boss' (Sir Matt Busby) kept repeating 'We cannot play on this. We just cannot play.'

52

Sir Matt Busby (centre) *putting new life into Manchester United before the start of extra time in the European Cup Final against Benfica*

Bobby Charlton (No. 9) shows his jubilation after scoring Manchester United's first goal against Benfica in the European Cup Final at Wembley. May, 1968

Goal No. 2 for Manchester United against Gornik at Old Trafford

George Best (right) *in action against Gornik*

I remember saying that it would be a good pitch for us. 'No-one could score on a pitch like it' I argued, 'and as we have a 2–0 lead, that suits us just fine.'

As it happened, Gornik did score – just one, late on. It wasn't enough. We were on our way to Madrid and that memorable victory over

an integral part of the triumph and drawn into the celebrations.

So players like Denis Law, Francis Burns, David Herd, John Fitzpatrick and Jimmy Rimmer played a vital part throughout the whole of the European Cup competition.

This trophy wasn't won on one match alone –

The sporting side of the European Cup. Manchester United players applaud Gornik goalkeeper Kostka as he leaves the field

Real, and ultimately the emotion of Wembley.

I suppose that by now a million words have been written about this fantastic night. All too few of them however, have been about a major reason for our success . . . I refer to the players who didn't make the final team. But just as when England won the World Cup, the eleven reserve members of the pool were accepted as

it was a team effort over many months and in many lands. These players deserved the gold medals, struck specially for them, just as much as the eleven players who bestrode Wembley on that May night.

What sort of agonies I wonder, did Jimmy Rimmer go through. Every match right through to the final, this fine yet inexperienced young

55

goalkeeper had to sit on the touchline wondering if he might be called on because a goalkeeper could be substituted at any time. So at any moment he could have had to step out into a crisis. Had Alex Stepney been hurt, Jimmy would have been plunged into the fiercest of competitions. With hardly an hour in the first-team jersey to give him confidence, he would have become the most vital member of the side at the most crucial time. It is difficult to understand just how he felt – although Bobby Charlton and myself had our own problems AFTER we had won the cup.

That May night provided us with our greatest honour, our greatest thrill and for me the most emotional night I have ever known. Yet it was such a bad one for Bobby and me. We both had to forget the celebrating and go straight to bed. We were shattered, emotionally ill, physically sick. It was all right while we were playing even during extra time. But afterwards . . .

Perhaps it was the passion and desire to win, the great effort of concentration, maybe even the disappointment and the anger that overwhelmed us at one stage, when we let Benfica back into the game.

People said later that we faded badly. I think that, although Mr Busby had hammered away at us not to be complacent.

We all remembered our great 5–1 win over Benfica in Lisbon two years before. We tended to think that when we had one goal it was enough. It wasn't, of course. We let Benfica back, and they equalized and we faced extra time.

That was when Nobby Stiles lifted us all. Normally when he is angry Nobby is a funny little man.

Now, as we waited to see what the extra anxious thirty minutes would bring, he stormed at us. 'You've thrown it away', he raged. And then he spoke the vital words that may well have won us the Cup: 'You think you're tired . . . well, that team over there is twice as tired'.

This time we didn't laugh at an angry Nobby . . . we went out to win the Soccer crown of Europe.

Then, for Bobby and me, came the let-down. Neither of us attended the official celebrations; Jack Crompton, our coach realized the terrible state we were in and spoke to the Boss. We were allowed back to our hotel to bed.

I felt a little better around 3 o'clock in the morning and I thought I should join the party down below.

In a while I chatted to the relatives of the lads lost at Munich. It was pleasant and touching, and I would not have wanted to miss it. But after one 'coke' – believe me or believe me not, my total intake that night of long celebration – I was ill again.

And so I returned to my bed to suffer the worst night of my life. Not until Friday, after our return to that fantastic welcome in Manchester, did I begin to feel anything like normal again. How Bobby felt or managed having to join the England team on the Thursday morning, I shall never know.

Anyway, Manchester United proved themselves the Kings of Europe. Yet I do not believe we were the best United team in Europe. We had a better one that never won the European Cup – the 1965 side. That one, badly hit by the injury to George Best lost to Partizan. But I still believe that it was the best balanced side the club has had. Not the best individuals, but the best balanced side . . .

Harry Gregg, Shay Brennan, Tony Dunne, myself, Bill Foulkes, Nobby Stiles, John Connelly, Bobby Charlton, David Herd, Denis Law, and Georgie, of course.

You may not agree.

Another team may yet win the European Cup again. To have won it once was a dream come true; now I would be satisfied to do it just once more!

56

Kilmarnock v. *Aberdeen. Surrounded by Kilmarnock players Dons' 'keeper McGarr punches the ball over the bar for a corner.* Left to right: *Murray (Aberdeen) McIlroy and Morrison (Kilmarnock), McGarr and Queen (Kilmarnock)*

This Might Have Been Des O'Connor's Football Book

says Des O'Connor

I'M mad about football. Frankly, I don't get enough time to watch or play it as often as I would like. That's why I'm only too happy to be writing in *John Greig's Annual* for I have a great admiration for his stylish play.

What is more, if fate had so decreed, I might have been a star footballer myself. You see when I was ill, my family was evacuated from Stepney in the East End of London and we moved to Northampton. That was during the blitz of the 1939–45 war when so many people were moved from bomb-scarred London.

In those days I was so small that Jimmy Clitheroe could have played my father in pantomime! Then, when I was fifteen, I shot up almost overnight. In fact, I was so tall I couldn't get in to see Northampton Town as a boy any more!

Yes, I was mad on football even then. I found that I wasn't a bad player at all and when some friends suggested I apply to Northampton – affectionately known as the Cobblers – for a trial, I did just that. You can imagine how de-

lighted I was when I was signed on as an amateur and found myself playing on the wing for the Colts.

Unfortunately, I wasn't quite good enough or heavy enough and when National Service caught up with me and I joined the RAF, that was the end of my aspirations as a footballer. But I've never lost interest in the fortunes of Northampton and Dave Bowen, the manager, is a great friend of mine. Whenever I visit my

Des O'Connor (left) *before a match.*
Picture: Bournemouth Times Series

Kilmarnock 'keeper Sandy McLauchlan punches the ball clear from his own centre-half Jack McGroy and left-half Frank Beattie standing by in the background

parents at the weekend I always try to see the Cobblers and I would dearly like to see them win some of the great football prizes.

I suppose it's natural that people like myself should have such an affinity with soccer. Most of the comics I know love to see a football match and football players are always welcome backstage. Mike and Bernie Winters are dedicated soccer fans and they play a lot of football too. Back in 1967 they put in a bid to buy Aston Villa. It was Bernie's idea. He reckoned if he ever wanted his teeth out he needn't go to the dentist – he could just stand in front of the goal during practice! Another footballing mate of mine, Stan Stennett, also had some dealings with the Villa in 1968 when he offered to form a show-biz consortium to take over the club. Not such a bad idea when you come to think of it. After all, Stan could always get some advice from his great friend Trevor Ford, one-time Villa and Wales player.

Stan is also a pilot and flies his plane all over the country. He told me that once he was flying Trevor back from London when they got caught in a storm and had to make a forced landing. It was very tricky at the time, but when they were safe on terra firma Stan made a quip of the unhappy experience: 'Well, Trevor,' he said, 'You nearly died with your footballing boots on.'

Eric Morecambe and Ernie Wise are two more pals who enjoy their soccer. Eric supports Luton Town and Ernie goes to see Peterborough play whenever he can. They don't actively play football, but they like table soccer and often play local teams when they're appearing in the provinces. Jimmy Tarbuck and Mike Yarwood also enjoy a game of football and play a lot for charity matches. And Ken Dodd, who supports Liverpool F.C. is also an unpaid, unofficial scout for the club. He has recommended more Diddymen than anybody else in the game, but with players getting taller, it's difficult to place them.

This is why I believe that there ought to be more co-operation between our two branches of entertainment. As soccer is such an important part of people's entertainment, surely the customers could be as well-looked after as are the people who come to see us in the theatre. I would like to see footballers projected more on television; give them a chance to prove that they are personalities, many of them with as much character as the Freddie Trueman's of this world. Most of us only know a soccer star by his play on the field or what we read in the sporting pages of our newspapers. Why can't we have a look behind the scenes and see what really makes him tick (or should it be kick!)

Nowadays, soccer players are better paid than they've ever been and many of them are now wise enough to invest in a job for the future. Players such as George Best who has a boutique, Ronnie Simpson a sports shop, while Billy McNeill and John Greig have a number of business interests.

These players have spent their spare time in building up commercial ventures realizing that they have only a limited period in which to cash in on their footballing skill. But all of them still put soccer first, no matter what business commitments they have. They are wise enough to know that without their soccer skill – and the cash it brings – they wouldn't be able to devote time to building up outside interests.

It's the same in my business. I have invested in a number of enterprises, but I still regard entertaining as my prime job. My outside interests are an insurance for the future and it is this knowledge of a certain amount of security which makes me enjoy my work all the more.

One of the great differences in my type of entertaining and soccer is the people who watch. I don't mean those who sit at home and watch us on television, but the people who pay to come into the theatres and clubs and who pay to stand on the terraces or sit in the seats. Most entertainers in my line of show-biz get a very fair hearing; sometimes there's the odd barracker in a club, but if you can give him a smart answer, you usually come out on top.

But in soccer, it only needs a minority hooligan element and the whole game can be spoiled. I enjoy the verbal cut and thrust of opposing fans, but I deplore the bad language which so often creeps into an argument and I despise the few who make a great game undignified by throwing toilet rolls on to the pitch and vent their feelings by smashing windows to and from the ground. These hooligans need stopping so that the real soccer lovers can enjoy their game in peace.

Little do they realize that they are doing soccer and their club a great dis-service. At a time when every possible outsider should be lured to watch football games, this sort of behaviour keeps would-be fans at home. Why should a boy or a girl, a man or a woman, risk being seriously hurt through attending a football game? It's a problem which supporters must solve themselves. Otherwise, I can see the time when even smaller gates will be the accepted pattern, with more and more clubs going into bankruptcy.

But enough of this serious discourse by Desmond. Football is a great game and I enjoy every minute of it. I've played with show-biz teams ever since they were formed and it has given me the opportunity not only of playing alongside some of my fellow entertainers, but with such football greats as Billy Wright and Len Duquemin.

I can remember playing for the Show-Biz XI against a police team at Barnet. We won 3–2 and I scored a hat trick! I was as pleased with this achievement as when my first record 'Careless Hands' went into the Hit Parade. Of course, sometimes the games aren't all that serious such as the time I played at Bournemouth in a team of summer entertainers which included Jack Douglas and Kenneth McKellar who played in a kilt! Mrs Mills, that amiable pianist kicked off. We played against the Bournemouth police and the result was a 5–5 draw.

It's a long time since I appeared in Scotland, but when I do, I hope that someone will ask me to play against a charity team. And if John Greig should happen to be on the opposite side, I'll ask him to autograph this article!

The goal that put St. Mirren back on the winning trail. Peter Kane slams the ball past Clyde goalkeeper John Wright to give Saints their first win in five games. December, 1968

The Human Side of Football

by George McLean

I'M football's unluckiest fella, the guy who gets caught every year between the Old Firm fans – the followers of Celtic and Rangers.

I'm the player they love to boo, the player who is singled out at Celtic Park and Ibrox for special attention.

I get the boos at Celtic Park because I once played for Rangers and the Celtic fans obviously still look on me as a Rangers' player . . .

I get the boos at Ibrox because the fans there still blame me for the Scottish Cup defeat to a Second Division side Berwick Rangers at Berwick a few seasons back . . .

All of which makes it a complicated set-up for me when all I want to do is get on with my new career which is at Dundee.

When I first moved, of course, as part of a transfer deal when Rangers signed Andy Penman from Dundee, I wanted to prove to the Ibrox club and to the fans that they had made a mistake about me. I think I succeeded when I scored thirty-five goals in that first season at Dens Park.

And now I find that I can relax – which is something I could never do when I played for Rangers. In the five years I was at Ibrox – I joined them for a £27,000 fee from my local team in Paisley, St Mirren – I rarely felt able to enjoy my football. There was a constant strain on me and on the entire team, the kind of strain that few teams ever experience or even realize exists. Our fans honestly expected us to win every week. If we didn't then they wanted players to be dropped and I became one of their favourite targets . . .

I suppose, of course, that this is part of the trouble of being a striker in the modern game. If you fail to get goals then you have failed in your main job. People on the terraces are only too ready to write you off, to get you out of the team. And I know that most strikers are like myself. Once you have had a bad run and the fans begin to barrack you a bit, then your confidence grows less and less and your form worse and worse. When confidence goes then you don't want to take a crack at goal for yourself, you begin to look around for someone else – anyone else – to pass the ball to rather than try yourself. You never improve that way unless

63

'You beaut!' Colin Stein might be saying as he scores the winning goal for Rangers against his former club, Hibs

Colin Jackson, full-back with the striker's touch, has done it again . . . Right-winger Willie Johnston and his jubilant inside man Alex Ferguson rush to congratulate Jackson (on the ground) after his overhead kick had clinched a 2–0 win for Rangers against Morton

65

George McLean

Jimmy Johnston, Celtic's right-winger, and Jim Easton, Dundee's centre-half, in a race for the ball at Parkhead

just once you hit it right again, then your lost form can miraculously return . . .

The Rangers' fans were often too demanding. I don't find the support the same at Dens Park from that viewpoint. Yet, on the other hand, when you were playing well that vast Rangers' support could inspire you to even greater things.

For instance, you never feel that you are playing an away game when you are with Rangers or Celtic, too, I suppose. The huge travelling support that goes with the Big Two to every game often outnumbers the home support at the other grounds. It gives both the big Glasgow teams a tremendous advantage, one that no other team in Britain can claim.

I know that Manchester United and Liverpool and other top English teams can command large numbers of travelling supporters. But, in Scotland, the distances the fans have to travel are much smaller and it is very much easier to follow your team week after week. And, don't forget the fans of Celtic and Rangers come from all parts of Scotland. I knew that when I was at Ibrox, but it has been brought home to me more forcibly now, that I play for a provincial club like Dundee because every Saturday we can see Celtic and Rangers' fans leave the city in busloads to watch their teams either in action in Glasgow or elsewhere. For really important games the travelling support can be around thirty thousand!

That is the type of thing you find yourself up against when you leave one of the Old Firm club to play for a lesser known team. I have found it more than anyone else because, as I said at the beginning, I get a hot reception from these fans. Fortunately I don't let that worry me too much. It did when I was playing for Rangers, but now I look on the boos in a different way. When I was with Rangers I knew the fans were picking on me – my OWN fans. Now, they are the other fans and if they boo me, then I take it as a bit of a compliment. Maybe they are a little worried about what I might do

against them, for instance. I mean that. I've had better games for Dundee against Celtic than I ever had for Rangers against Celtic.

And now when I come up against Rangers in any game I play as hard as I know how . . .

I'm still friendly with quite a few of the lads at Ibrox, particularly Willie Henderson and Ronnie McKinnon, but that doesn't affect me at all when I'm on the field playing against them. They are just like any other players then. Like every other player, once you are out on the field all you want to do is help your team to win a game . . . though naturally when you come up against your mates a bit of kidding can go on – like in one game the other season when we were playing against Rangers at Dens Park, and I went for a high ball with Ronnie McKinnon. Now, at Ibrox we used to kid Ronnie on about the care he took over his appearance. So when I went for this ball my elbow accidentally caught him on the nose. Then when the ball broke from us and was at the other end of the field I almost burst out laughing when a voice behind me said: 'Here, big man, watch the good looks!' It was Ronnie, living up to all the dressing-room jokes we had made over the years at Ibrox.

The game is full of incidents like that one, always proving that there is a human side no matter how professional your approach. We may look as if we hate the sight of each other for ninety minutes . . . but it isn't really as bad as that at all.

Sometimes, though, I miss the atmosphere that we had at the big games at Ibrox. I feel that if we could get that at Dens Park, and I didn't have the strain I suffered from at Ibrox, then I would be 100 per cent happy with my game.

When the crowd is big I feel that I have the ability to rise to the occasion. Somehow a lot of the players in the Dundee team are the same. We did it in our Fairs Cities Cup games in my first season with the club. In the first round, for instance, when we beat Liege 4–1 in Belgium and I grabbed all four of our goals. We reached the semi-finals only to be beaten by the odd goal in three by Leeds United, who went on to win the Cup. For these Fairs games we had bigger than usual crowds coming to Dens Park and we were able to lift our game to get good results – the results we wanted.

It made me think that if every provincial team could raise their game on big occasions, as we did for these games, then the League challenge to the Old Firm would be more formidable. Unfortunately, talking from my own experience, too many teams playing against Rangers fall apart once the Ibrox team have taken the lead. That doesn't make for a healthy League competition. We need more effort from every team – and I include my own team here – to get a strong League.

I hope it happens. Whether it does or not, I do know one thing that will happen . . . I'll be barracked by the Old Firm fans whenever I play in front of them and it won't upset me one little bit.

So near . . . yet so far! McKenzie (Aidrie) gets down to the ball in time to thwart Rangers. Can you name the other players in the picture?

It's Fun Learning to Play

by Roy Small

Lecturer at Jordanhill P.E. College and Manager of Scottish Youth Team

For many Scottish boys football means total involvement, an involvement which might mean fun, freedom and excitement with their school pals or perhaps even the splendours of Hampden, Wembley or ultimately playing in the magnificent Stadium of Light in Lisbon, home of the renowned BENFICA. The goal that brings the thunder of a hundred thousand voices might mean no more than the one scored in the wind, rain and dusk of the local pitch. It's the tension, excitement and satisfaction that counts for us all – it is playing which brings that and it is playing that counts.

Playing in the park and in the school, from the primary, senior and through into the serious commitment of youth football, where the marks of talent or even greatness begin to show. Talent that might be even slow to show – but when it does it is time to move on and find an outlet perhaps in the intense competitive world of the professional game.

What are these qualities which boys begin to show which stamp them as being special – different – uniqueness which is theirs alone, that can make them a vital part of a great team? It could be the elusive, deceptive, quicksilver penetration of Jimmy Johnstone of Celtic, the composed, thoughtful, tenacious angling and passing skill of Tom Craig of Aberdeen, or the stand firm, dourness, strength and destructive determination of a defender like John Greig.

Whatever qualities you have will come out according to your personality and ability. What you must do is to play and to practice with determination to make the best possible use of your natural ability – play again and again – develop it.

Perhaps some day you will join one of the big clubs, then your skill will be used to make your *team* a great one. Your coach will mould your skill, together with that of your teammates, to shape the tactics of your team, since tactics can only evolve out of skill.

You will be trained in many different ways to develop your *Speed*, *Strength*, *Endurance*, *Agility* and *Skill*.

Football is a game of infinite variety. In some teams we have the 'beautiful game' of the Spanish Real Madrid and the Central European countries, perhaps modelled on the old Scottish

69

game of quick passing and interpassing, played at high speed with exciting fluid movement – in others the accurate, dynamic long ball thrusts through to quick-striking players, coupled with weaving, dribbling wing-men penetrating down the line and through the middle. Both can be tremendously stimulating and exciting, depending on the players you have in your team.

Some teams are strong physically and use hard vigorous contact with their technique – it is an important part of the game and it is part of the thrilling, unpredictable nature of football that on some days strength wins, and on others, skill. Build your game on what you have.

In shaping the team – once the basic fitness is established – provide the freedom, by sound defence, to let the players express their natural, inherent skill in attack: good defensive play will give a wonderful opportunity for spontaneous attacking play. Who can say that W.M., 4 : 2 : 4, 4 : 3 : 3 or Cattenachio are the last word in playing systems? Young players and original coaches will bring new techniques and flair to the game.

The good coach will know and grow with his players, working on the individual strengths, not changing their normal habits and responses but shaping them together to get the best possible striking force.

Some players have team sense – others do not – it is the player with team sense who must adjust his game to bring out the best in those who don't. The individual is all important, because great individuals make great teams but they must play in a team secure enough to let the ability flourish.

Develop your own skill individually and in co-operation with others. Remember this – the first aim in football is to score goals – the second to prevent goals being scored against you.

Get possession of the ball – keep it as a group – practice in small groups receiving the

70

ball – turning and screening the ball to make an angle for your pass – with the correct strength and accuracy – running to support the new player with the ball.

To practice you don't always have to play a full game of 11 *v.* 11.

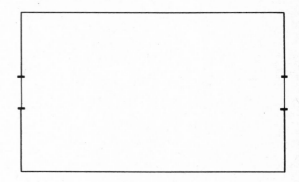

Try these small games with your pals, set out a small pitch like this:

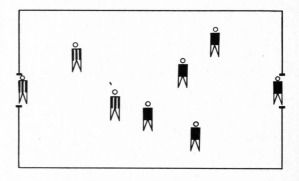

The size is not too important – about **40 yds.** long by **25 yds.** wide and have goals at each end.

Try this practice with goalkeepers in
4 players *v.* 2 players.

The four boys with the ball are trying to score goals by interpassing movements – try to make square passes, setting up passes followed by through passes – the two players are trying to defend their goal by interception and zoning and when they get possession, hit long shots at the opposing goalkeeper.

The goal that caused the storm at Parkhead. Bobby Lennox taps the ball into the net as Bobby Clark turns to protest to the referee

Now, using the same field, make it more difficult for the strong side by playing 3 *v.* 2 – this is much more like the actual game – try to keep possession and finish with a goal.

Go on from there, take turns of playing 2 *v.* 1 on the field – practice wall passes – if you cannot make a wall pass like this

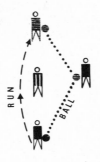

Practice running in, against the defender, turning and passing the ball to your partner who will then return the ball for you to run on to – by playing tight against your opponent, you will prevent him intercepting the ball and you can go on to score.

Now try to develop your technique in running with the ball and beating your opponent.

Watch how

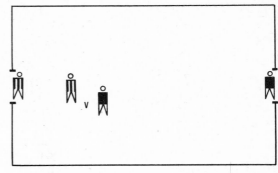

The goalkeeper throws or kicks the ball and the mid-field players challenge for possession – then the dribbling to get within scoring range begins. Always try to finish the practice by having a game – during the 5 *v.* 5 or 6 *v.* 6 games depending on how many of you there are – practise the following:

1. Passing whenever you can to one of your team-mates.
2. Go and help the man who has the ball by getting close to him to receive a pass.
3. Keep the ball moving.
4. Only drive in for a shot at goal when you are within scoring distance.

Goals are vitally important – but so also is playing together. Pass – run – play together to score goals – who knows what the future holds!

Tommy Callaghan, Celtic F.C.

*Dunfermline goalkeeper Bent Martin gathers the ball as Tommy McLean (Kilmarnock)
runs in to challenge and centre-half Roy Barry covers up*

*Celtic v. Kilmarnock. Johnstone watches his shot go past with only left-back Billy
Dickson between him and glory. Killie's Jim McLean watches anxiously*

A great save by St. Mirren 'keeper Thornburn foils the eager Partick Thistle forwards.
Saints went on to beat Thistle 2–0

Aberdeen centre-half McMillan clears the ball from Kilmarnock's outside-left McIlroy
and his Dons team-mate Whyte

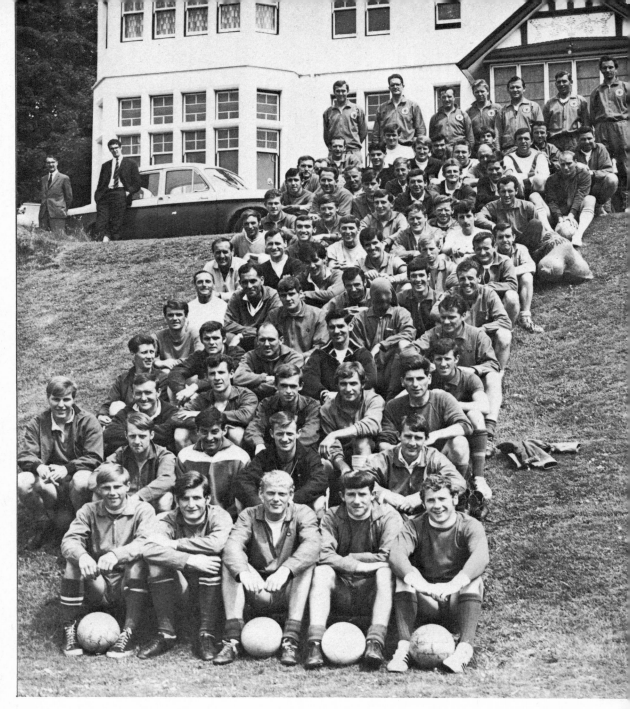

This is a picture of the Scottish Football Association's coaching course held at the National Centre, Inverclyde. Roy Small is second from the left on the top row of coaches and Altham Turner, Principal of Inverclyde, is in the top left-hand corner

Inverclyde National Recreation Centre, Largs

by Altham Turner, Principal

THE eyes of the World were focused on Mexico for the 1968 Olympic Games.

The miracles of science and, in particular, the advances made in transmitting pictures now enable all of us to have a ringside seat at these international contests as they happen. Thanks to television and satellites, for the duration of the Games, those of us prepared and able to sit up until the small hours could see many world-shattering feats. What a thrill to see the phenomenal leap of long jumper, Bob Beaman, the curious technique and style of Dick Fosbury, to mention but two; to say nothing of the pride we felt in the performances of our medal winners. Enthusiasts of all sports united to salute athletes David Hemery, Sheila and John Sherwood and Lillian Board, boxer Chris Finnegan, crack shot Bob Braithwaite with a fantastic 198 out of 200 score, sailors Rodney Pattison and Ian McDonald Smith and last, but not least, riders Major Derek Allhusen, Miss Jane Buller, Mr Richard Meade, Sgt. Jones, David Broome, Marion Coakes and the unforgettable Stroller.

In 1970 Mexico will once again be the centre of world-wide interest – The World Cup.

Wembley Stadium has room for some 100,000 spectators but countless millions throughout the world saw the final between England and West Germany in 1966. And now the pot is beginning to boil again. Because of the large number of countries now taking part in the competition, preliminary hurdles have to be overcome before a team can find a place in the final stages. Only England, as the present holders, and Mexico, as the host country, automatically go forward to Mexico.

Team managers throughout the world are wrestling with two problems – one, to produce a team capable now of securing a place in the Mexico pool, and secondly, to build a team to play and win in 1970.

Football fans in Scotland, second to none in their knowledge of the game, and their enthusiasm for it, were disappointed their team failed to qualify for the final games in England in 1966. They watch, with very deep interest, every move along the long and difficult road to Mexico.

The fans have noticed that, for a year or two

now, the international squad have gathered at Inverclyde, the National Sports Training Centre for pre-international match preparation.

INVERCLYDE!!

Scotland's National Recreation Centre was established by the Scottish Council of Physical Recreation in 1958 as a memorial to King George VI with a grant from the King George VI Foundation.

The centre is most attractively situated, standing high in its own grounds in an estate of seventy-eight acres, overlooking the beauti-ful Ayrshire seaside town of Largs. It has a magnificent view to the front of the Firth of Clyde, the Cumbraes, Arran and Bute. Behind the centre is open moorland, hills and lochs. There is easy access from large centres of population by bus and train, Glasgow being approximately one hour's journey.

The large residence has been adapted to provide first-class accommodation for about ninety people with comfortable lounges and lecture rooms. The sports facilities have been developed over the years to provide the finest

Willoughby (Rangers) slips the ball past Mulhearson of Clyde

Up goes Rangers centre-forward Colin Stein . . . But he came off second best in this goal-mouth duel with Hearts 'keeper Jim Cruikshank, who managed to punch the ball clear

possible training conditions for most games and sports.

Out of doors there is a sports field where pitches for football, rugby, hockey, lacrosse, and other field games can be laid out. Alongside is an all-weather 'blaes' area which can be used for most games and is also used as an athletics training area. Another facility is the 'Tennisquick' area, an all-weather, non-attention surface, which provides excellent conditions for many games and, in particular, tennis. This area is floodlit.

The Sports Hall can cater for a variety of activities. Big enough for two tennis or two basketball courts, it can also be used for football training when the weather is bad. A smaller hall is ideal for sports like Fencing, Judo, Weight-lifting, and there are Squash Courts, an exercise room and lecture rooms.

There is a riding school, indoor golf nets and a fleet of boats to take advantage of the wonderful sailing conditions the Clyde offers.

What happens at Inverclyde?

It is firstly a Centre – it might also be called a College – for the training of coaches and instructors in all games and sports, fencing leaders, weight-lifting instructors, and of course, football coaches. Different sports have different names but all are now very active in training coaches and none more than the Scottish Football Association.

In late June and early July each year the Scottish Football Association is busy with coaching courses. These are arranged for footballers of all grades who want to become coaches. They include teachers, who want to raise standards in school; Boys' Clubs; Youth, Junior and Amateur representatives keen to keep up with the latest developments; and professional players hoping to remain in the game when their playing days are finished.

Secondly, the wonderful facilities of Inverclyde are used by the Scottish sports bodies for the training of selected players for special events, including international fixtures. Just as

Scottish athletes, boxers, fencers, badminton players, wrestlers and weight-lifters gather to prepare for the 1970 Commonwealth Games in Edinburgh, so the Scottish Team gather prior to their Hampden games.

Other sports bodies, the Scottish Lawn Tennis Association, for example, gather promising young players – as young as 10, 11, or 12 – for special coaching under Bill Moss, the national coach.

Whether for promising youngsters, or established stars, or for stages between the two, most sports use Inverclyde for these top level training sessions.

The third way Inverclyde helps with the development of sport in Scotland is by arranging special courses for Training College students and others, including a small number of school children, aimed at introducing them to new activities.

And so Inverclyde is busy throughout the year with a programme covering most games and sports.

With shorter working weeks we are all now beginning to get more time with which to enjoy games and sports both as player and spectator and, with increased opportunity has come greater freedom of choice and also a greater awareness of the high standards of performance in the world today.

Whatever we do, wherever we play, whenever we watch, there is a growing demand for more and better teachers or coaches and for better facilities. This is why the Scottish Council of Physical Recreation established the National Recreation Centre at Inverclyde.

Football is a popular game played and watched by millions and nowhere in the world can knowledge and enthusiasm match that of the Scots.

1970 will indeed be a year of years for football fans, particularly those supporters whose team wins the coveted World Cup. Will 1970 be Scotland's year? Whatever the outcome, in the background will be the contribution made

81

Dundee United 'keeper MacKay punches clear in the match against Dunfermline

by Inverclyde, and the Scottish team when it does win will contain players who were first taught by coaches who trained at Inverclyde, players who first trained at Inverclyde as members of the Scottish Association of Boys' Clubs' squad, and players who graduated from the Youth XI to the Under-23 side.

We would all like to see this happen in 1970 and with world-class stars like John Greig, Denis Law, Jimmy Johnston, Billy Bremner, Bobby Murdoch in the squad, hopes must be high and prospects bright. Celtic has given the lead at club level – Scotland will not lack support for her efforts in Mexico in 1970.

Willie Mathieson and John Greig of Rangers stop Willie Hamilton of Hearts from going through with the ball

82

Ronnie McKinnon of Glasgow Rangers

'The first man I want to mention' writes Ronnie Simpson 'is the late Frank Swift who must always be classed among the goalkeeping greats'

Goalkeepers

by Ronnie Simpson

THE question I'm most often asked by fans is, who were my own special favourites among all the goalkeepers I have seen.

It's never a question that annoys me in the least . . . in fact, it's one that I like to have asked. I enjoy talking about my favourite 'keepers just as anyone likes to talk about the top men in his particular profession. So, here, I've decided to make a list of my main favourites – with some mention of the qualities that they had or have, that made them special to me.

I haven't attempted to put them in any order of merit. I don't want to do that because in my opinion they are all bracketed so closely together that it would be unfair to single out any one player as the greatest goalkeeper I have ever seen.

You might be surprised, after reading my listing, to find that I haven't named many Continental goalkeepers – except, of course, for the giant Russian Lev Yashin. This is simply because I believe you must see goalkeepers several times before you can form firm opinions on their abilities.

Anyhow, to get on with it, the first man I want to mention is the late Frank Swift who must always be classed among the goalkeeping greats. I was pretty young when I was watching Swift in action but even so I remember being envious of the natural advantages he had over so many other goalkeepers.

He had such tremendous height and reach and it must have been frightening for a forward coming in on goal to look up and see Frank filling the goalmouth. Frank had the physical attributes that I, for one, don't have. Coming out for a high ball was child's play to him because of his height and weight while the rest of us have to fight hard against forwards coming in to challenge.

There are a couple of goalkeepers from Scotland that deserve special mention in any list of mine . . . Jerry Dawson and Bobby Brown. So, here am I, a Celtic player, choosing two men from Rangers!

Dawson had everything a goalkeeper should have. He had many outstanding qualities yet at the same time none of them overshadowed the others. He was perfectly co-ordinated, brave and agile.

85

'It's mine – and I'm keeping it!' Ronnie Simpson shows all the determination that's made him Scotland's top goalkeeper as Ian Stewart of Clyde challenges

'England's World Cup goalkeeper, Gordon Banks, reminds me a bit of Frank Swift' says Ronnie Simpson. Here Banks is first to the ball in an England v. Scotland match at Hampden Park

'Perhaps that's why there are good young goalkeepers down South, because so much more is demanded from them. I think particularly of Gordon West (here seen in action for Everton against Newcastle) and Peter Springett as well as Bonetti when I say this'

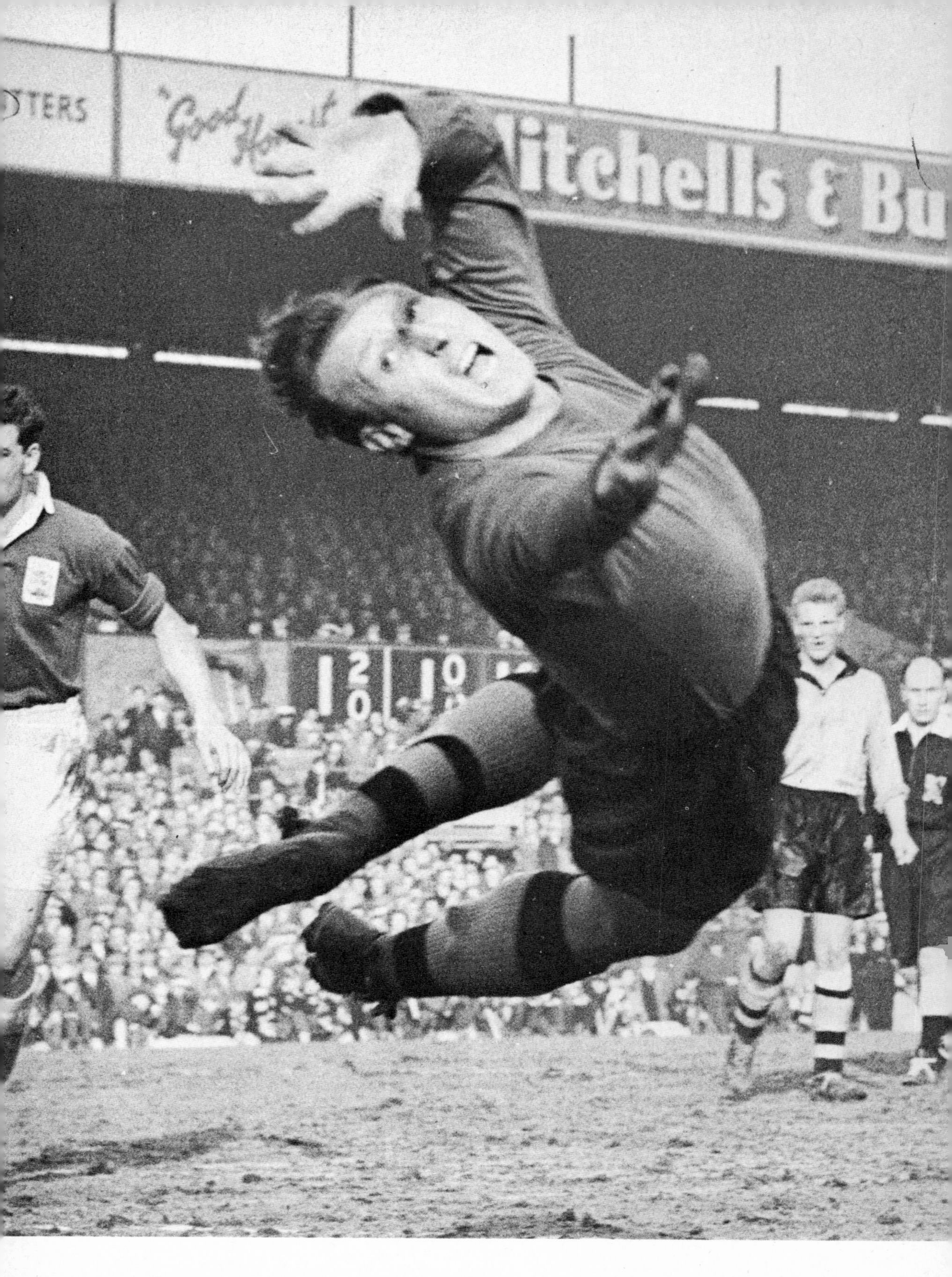

The other, Bobby Brown, is now Scotland's team manager and the man who gave me my first international cap at the age of thirty-six. He was also the regular first team 'keeper for Queen's Park when I started playing for them as a youngster of fourteen.

Bobby was often under-estimated as a 'keeper. He was very lithe and I always remember his amazingly accurate kicking with his left foot. That made a big impression on me then· Accurate kicking by a goalkeeper can be tremendously important to any team in helping them to start attacks. Bobby practised this, and I tried to learn from him . . . it was a valuable lesson.

Most of the 'keepers I do admire are English 'keepers – some from the days when I played myself for Newcastle United. Bert Williams and Ron Springett for example right to the present day and Peter Bonetti and Gordon Banks.

And somehow I find that the men I most admire are the men who had the same physical problems as myself . . . a bit on the small side for a goalkeeper and possibly too slightly built to stand up to the powerful forwards in the English First Division.

Take that fabulous Wolves' star, Bert Williams. He was only around five feet nine inches or so tall and when he played there were a whole lot of top-class 'keepers around yet Bert more than held his own. He had absolutely amazing agility. I know there were times when I thought to myself how much I was handicapped by lack of inches and how I would like extra height – like Swift I suppose – and I know that Bert must have thought the same. But the important thing was that Bert worked on other departments of his game to make up for the lack of inches.

The more recent England 'keeper, Ron Springett, is another example of this. Again he is on the small side but he has strength. I will always remember how Ron would come off his line for a high ball, and the determination he

'The other Bobby Brown, is now Scotland's team manager and the man who gave me my first international cap'

showed in getting up with forwards who were maybe two or three inches taller than himself. Yet Ron would go up with two of them and come down holding the ball so safely. I saw him play some great games. . . .

Nowadays Peter Bonetti is the man I like to watch most. He is acrobatic and so fast at moving to a ball too. Besides that I always have the impression that Bonetti can read the game marvellously well.

England's World Cup goalkeeper, Gordon Banks, reminds me a bit of Frank Swift. He seems to fill the goal the way Swift used to do

89

'Take that fabulous Wolves' star, Bert Williams . . . He had absolutely amazing agility' (*as this picture shows*)

'Yashin, the Russian, is another good big one. His punching is one particularly impressive feature of his game.' Here Yashin is seen in action in the Russia v. Italy World Cup match in 1966

'Nowadays Peter Bonetti is the man I like to watch most'

. . . but he doesn't have Bonetti's agility. And, also, he plays more on his line than the other players I have mentioned.

Yashin, the Russian, is another good big one. His punching is one particularly impressive feature of his game. I know that a lot of people think that goalkeepers should always try to clutch high balls when they come into goal. But with Yashin that cannot be right. He punches with tremendous timing and can send the ball so far.

I had to work on this department myself when I was with Newcastle. In those days when the goalkeeper received less protection than now from the referees, you could find yourself in a bit of trouble if you tried to clutch a ball on the six-yards line as opposing centre-forwards came at you. I always felt it was better to punch the ball away rather than lose it a challenge. Some men didn't have the problem. For example, Swift didn't – and Springett managed to overcome it in another way.

I reckon, of course, that it's harder for a goalkeeper to play in English football, even though the more defensive set-ups mean less work. This defensive plays brings its own problems. It makes it much easier for you to be caught cold by a snap shot after spending a long long time doing nothing . . .

That makes it as hard a job today as it ever was. Goalkeepers have to be on their toes even more because of the element of surprise; the possibility of being caught unawares is more than ever a danger.

Perhaps that's why there are good young goalkeepers down South, because so much more is demanded from them. I think particularly of Gordon West and Peter Springett as well as Bonetti when I say this.

England are fortunate to have so many 'keepers, disproving completely the theory that defensive football can kill the skills that make a great goalkeeper.

Anyhow, these are the men I have found something about which to admire. At times, indeed, the men I have been able to learn one or two things from, though the most important thing I ever learned was that you cannot model yourself completely on one man. You have to work things out for yourself. What was right for Frank Swift wasn't much use to a guy like me so many inches shorter. . . .

If there are any budding 'goalies' among you remember that.

Ready to test the 'keeper. Paul Stanton of Hibs in action against Rangers

Here's just one of Falkirk 'keeper Stewart Rennie's great saves against Celtic. He lies on the ground after punching a cross clear of Willie Wallace

Schools International match: England v. Scotland. Played at White Hart Lane, London, March 16th, 1968. Back row (left to right): R. Sherry (assistant team manager), A. Bruce, G. Souness, J. Harrower, T. Livingstone, A. Robertson, I. McHelam, R. Cairns, D. Macfarlane (team manager). Front row (left to right): M. Pollock, R. Miller, R. Gray, T. Sinclair, B. Laing, J. McGorley and J. Robertson

School's Football
in Scotland

by G. W. Newlands
Hon. Sec. Scottish Schools' F.A.

Last season almost 16,500 school matches were held in Scotland, 6,600 in Primary Schools and 9,900 in Secondary Schools and I hope you were playing in some of these matches.

There are forty-three District Associations throughout the country in membership of the Scottish Schools' Football Association, each District Association catering for the schools in its area by providing local league and cup competitions.

As you will appreciate, the strength of the National Association depends on the football played in the individual schools, added to the enthusiasm and hard work of the teachers who organize it at this level. In this respect special mention must be made of the difficult task carried out by the teachers in the Primary Schools where a start is made with the game on an organized basis. If you recall your first practice games, your sympathy should be with the ball as twenty little boys attacked it with great ferocity, the goalkeepers being restrained only with difficulty. It is only after much hard work

and many more practices that the idea of positional play and team work is instilled. In paying tribute to these teachers and also the ones who carry on the work in the Secondary Schools, it is important to stress that the glamour games, the schools' international matches played on senior grounds before large crowds, Wembley with its 90,000 spectators, would not be possible without them.

You may well ask what part the Scottish Schools' F.A. play in all this? It organizes competition on a national basis for individual schools and also for district associations, in addition to playing international matches.

In 1967–68, 155 schools entered for the Scottish Junior Shield. This competition is for Under-14 teams, and St Anthony's Secondary, Edinburgh and Woodlands Secondary, Falkirk contested the final which was played on a home and away basis. The first match at Falkirk produced a splendid contest with Woodlands up 3–1, inflicting the first defeat of the season on St Anthony's. The second leg was played at Easter Road and when Woodlands opened the scoring it seemed the trophy was going to Falkirk for the first time but a tremendous rally by St Anthony's resulted in a 4–1 win giving the Edinburgh school the trophy by an aggregate of 5–4.

The Scottish Intermediate Shield for Under-15 teams brought entries from 168 schools.

Bellshill Academy and Lawside Academy, Dundee were the finalists. In the first game at Dundee, Lawside were up 6–2 and although Bellshill tried hard in the second game at Fir Park Motherwell, Lawside were again successful by 3–1, thus winning this Shield by 9–3.

The Scottish Secondary Shield, the oldest of all school trophies presented by Queens Park F.C. in 1904, had ninety-six entries from schools with their Under-18 teams. By tradition the final is played at Hampden Park where Liberton Secondary, Edinburgh and Dalziel High, Motherwell fought out a hard exciting game ending with Liberton repeating their 1966 triumph by the only goal of the match.

For the Scottish Schools' Cup (Under-15) twenty-three districts entered. Ayrshire and Coatbridge & Airdrie contested the final. The first game, played at Somerset Park, Ayr, ended in a draw 2–2 and the second game at Broomfield Park, Airdrie was also a draw 1–1, the Cup being held jointly.

In the Wilson Trophy for the youngest boys, thirty-one districts entered their Under-12 teams. Dundee and Edinburgh won through to the final. At Dundee both teams served up a skilful and exciting match with the Edinburgh team being rather fortunate to win by 3–0. The Dundee boys opened the scoring at the second game played at Tynecastle Park, only to be defeated in the end by 2–1, Edinburgh winning the trophy by 5–1.

The aim of every schoolboy must be to play for his country and so receive an international cap. These matches are played at two age levels. Under-15 and Under-18. The Victory Shield for the Under-15 boys is the competition organized by the Schools' International Board for the

Home Countries – England, Ireland, Scotland and Wales. Each country plays every other country once in the season, the matches being arranged home one season and away the next. Points are awarded on a league basis. Goal average does not count towards winning the trophy, the Shield being shared in the event of more than one country obtaining the same number of points at the head of the table. The first of these matches was played against England in 1911, versus Wales in 1914 and versus Ireland in 1927.

The internationals for the older boys are a more recent innovation, the first being against England in 1955 while Wales entered this field in 1964.

The first international the season before last was for the Under-15 boys and was played at White Hart Lane, London against England. This was not a Victory Shield Match but an invitation match to celebrate the seventy-fifth anniversary of the London Schools' F.A. Before 15,000 spectators Scotland had a great start when Brian Laing, the Scottish centre-forward from Midlothian, headed a fine goal from a cross from the left. Although remaining on top for most of the game, the Scottish boys were unable to add to their total but finished worthy winners.

An unchanged team made the journey to Swansea on April 6 when – at Vetch Field – goals by Brian Laing and James McSorley (inside-left from Hamilton) gave Scotland a deserved victory over Wales by 2–0. This was a most encouraging start to the Victory Shield Competition.

A confident Scottish team set out to play Ireland at Londonderry on April 20 but hopes were dashed by a spirited Irish team which won deservedly by 3–1, the only Scottish goal being scored late in the game by Michael Carroll (outside-right from Aberdeen).

Scotland had thus to win the last international against England to have a chance of sharing the Championship. This was played at

It's Dundee United's second goal from Ian Mitchell against Dunfermline

Ibrox Park on May 11. The English team started off at a great pace and only the brilliance of Tom Livingstone (Glasgow) in goal kept the score sheet blank. Gradually, the Scottish boys took a grip of the game and again had to thank Brian Laing for scoring the only goal of the match. A fortnight later, England narrowly defeated Ireland 3–2 at South Shields and so the Victory Shield was shared.

On the same day as the match at Ibrox Park, the Under-18 team met England at Mansfield. The first half was evenly contested but a minute before the interval England opened the scoring and added a second goal almost immediately after the restart. This was a great blow to the Scottish team which never quite got on terms again with their opponents who eventually ran out 3–0 winners.

In the same series, Wales were the visitors at Cappielow Park, Greenock a week later. This looked a game which Scotland would win and hopes were high when James Whiteford (inside-left) from Airdrie scored the opening goal. The Scottish boys were well on top but poor finishing prevented them adding to their total. Near the end the Welsh centre-forward broke away to score the equalizing goal and almost immediately repeated the feat to score the winner a minute from time.

Played two, lost two was a most depressing record but there was some consolation when the team won the National Youth Competition by defeating the Boys' Club 4–2 in the final.

Like John Greig, most of our senior players started football at school and the present Scottish captain, Billy Bremner, played for the Scottish schools' team in 1958 in one of the finest school internationals ever to be played at Wembley. The Scottish team, down at one stage by five goals, rallied by Billy Bremner and scored three goals in the second half to make a recovery which was almost successful and which kept the 90,000 crowd shouting to the end.

Willie Johnstone takes a flying leap to head this cross from Persson in a Rangers v. Clyde match

So near . . . yet so far! Ritchie (Partick Thistle) saves at the feet of Lennox (Celtic) as Campbell and McKinnon keep their eyes on the ball

Boxing and Football

by Ken Buchanan

THERE are times when I meet my football pals, John Greig and Willie Henderson of Rangers, that I wonder if I would ever have made out as a professional footballer instead of a boxer.

Because there was a time in my teens when football ran boxing very close as my number one sport. I was playing inside forward then for an Edinburgh youth club team called United Cross Roads, the same team that John Greig played for when he was a kid. And the trainer of the team, Eric Gardner, wanted me to concentrate on football.

But eventually I had to make up my mind between the two sports and when I was nineteen I decided that I couldn't play football any longer. I was boxing as an amateur for Scotland at the time and really felt that I had to make up my mind to concentrate 100 per cent on the one sport.

You know, at that time I'd been doing double training stints every week. Two nights a week. I'd been with Eric Gardner training for football, then another three nights I'd be at my boxing club training for fights! It all became a bit too much.

Mind you, there are one or two training routines that work just as well for either sport . . . but there are others that just don't mix at all.

I always felt that the exercises we had for football helped me in my boxing. Footballers work very hard on building up their stomach muscles and this is important for boxers too.

So the things like press-ups were just as good for either sport. It was the running that was different. In football you have to concentrate on short sprints, quick bursts of speed that are essential to you in the games that you play.

In boxing that is all different. We have to work at distance running to help stamina. Every morning in my life I'm up early and off for a few miles along the Edinburgh roads. This helps us to last out a long fight . . . but it's absolutely no use to footballers.

I can verify this difference from personal experience. There was once, and it was after I had really given up playing for United Cross Roads, that Eric Gardner asked me if I would turn out for them. They were going to be a man short and they needed an inside forward. Well, I was keen to play. I had a fight coming up a

101

Ken Buchanan winning his bout with Phil Lundgen at the National Sporting Club, London. December 1966

week later but felt that if I kept clear of injury then there wouldn't be any problem. And, though I hadn't been training with Eric I had been working harder than ever before at the boxing club for this fight. I honestly had never felt fitter than I did that Saturday . . . yet within twenty minutes I was dead. I couldn't last the pace at all.

There I was 100-per-cent fit for a fight yet not able to play longer than twenty minutes full out in a football game . . . and it was only a juvenile game, at that!

Before the game that day I wouldn't have believed that there was so much difference between the types of fitness needed for the two sports. That really brought it home to me. When I was trying to use the short bursts needed for football my training, no matter how rigorous it had been, was no use.

Exactly the same kind of thing would happen if I'd been training with the football team and then been asked to fight. There are only slight differences in the routines but when it comes to actual practice then the differences are a whole lot greater than you would ever imagine.

As I said earlier, I had to choose between the two sports when I was nineteen . . . but I've never lost my liking for football. I still go to games and my family are all Hib's fans. We stayed in Easter Road and it was natural for us to go to the games there. The only thing now is that when I go to the games I never seem to see them playing too well . . . my father has told me I'm a jinx so I may just have to stay away.

Or else, I can repay the regular compliments that I get from my Ibrox pals and go to watch Rangers. It's always a boost to me when I fight down in London and see John Greig and Willie Henderson at the ringside. They are there whenever they can make it. The pair of them fly down, watch the fight then fly back to be in time for training the next morning.

Willie used to do a bit of boxing himself and I think that is why he is so keen. He's probably seen me fight even more than John has.

It's a funny thing, you know. John played for the youth club team before me yet it was only a few years ago that I actually met him.

Somehow or other I would arrive at the club one night and find that John had been the night before and Eric Gardner kept saying that we had just missed each other.

Then one night at a prize-giving we did get together and we've been friends ever since. John likes to talk to me about boxing and I like to talk to him about football. It keeps us both happy.

One of the advantages that the footballers have over me is the training facilities. They work with all the other players and under constant supervision . . . I train all alone. I used to travel to Wales and train under my manager Eddie Thomas but I didn't like being away from home so now I work out in Edinburgh and get local sparring partners. It's sometimes hard but being at home helps and I know just how much work I have to do to keep myself at peak fitness.

And after my experience a few years ago you won't catch me doing anything other than boxing training.

I've learned that lesson. Boxing and football at that level just don't mix.

Willie Henderson (Rangers) in action against Dundee United

World Cup–1970
by Billy McNeill

IT'S only a little over a year since I played in the fabulous Aztec Stadium in Mexico City . . . venue for the World Cup in 1970. I was there with my club Celtic, playing an unknown Mexico team in a tour game which, on paper, seemed all too easy for us. We lost . . . and at one time were three goals down to a team who would never have lived with us in Glasgow.

That was when it was brought home to me very forcibly just how hard it will be for a European team to win this coming World Cup.

We had gone to Mexico after playing two games in North America – in Toronto and New York – against the Italian champions AC Milan. Mexico City had been included in the short tour because Manager Jock Stein wanted to see how we reacted under the freakish altitude conditions.

The night before the game we trained and most of the lads felt all right. We had the club doctor there with us, and the atmosphere didn't seem too great a problem. At this stage we were more upset by the psychological worry that all the talk of altitude caused. There were times in

training – and the next night in the game, too – when we were apprehensive about going full out in case we suffered some kind of after-effects. Yet as the game itself went on we realized that you don't feel very much difference in sprints. The tightness across your chest comes after a long run . . . that's when you suffer!

This, too, can be helped by acclimatization. And the main problem that we had in our single game there can be cancelled out completely by experience. You see, we kept our routine before the game much the same as we have it at home. We sat down and ate a meal about a couple of hours before the kick-off – and that was our mistake. For most of the first half – the period when we lost three goals – we were sluggish. We simply couldn't get into our stride . . . and afterwards we found out why. A South American player who has played in Europe explained to us that the digestive processes take longer at that altitude. Instead of eating when we did, we should have had our mealtime brought forward several hours. This is what the Mexicans themselves do. It was a valuable lesson.

105

A fine action shot of Billy McNeill

England, of course, will plan meticulously in their effort to retain the trophy they won in 1966. They will be there in plenty of time to become acclimatized – and that will ease the worries. But it will *only* ease them. There are worry over the constantly changing venues. Home advantage has always been a very real advantage in the World Cup. Sweden, unknown and unrated reached the finals in their own country in 1958.

Celtic manager Jock Stein with the European Cup which Celtic won in 1967. On his desk are some of the telegrams he received from Britain's top football managers

other problems that the acclimatization cannot help . . . the way the ball moves in the air for instance. Because the atmosphere is rarefied, the ball comes at you quicker than usual and that takes some getting used to.

Even more than that will be the nagging

Then England won the Cup in 1966 playing all the games at Wembley. Now Mexico must be rated dangerous even though they would not be expected to reach the quarter-finals outside their own country.

For instance, Mexico can insist on playing

107

Wallace (Celtic) tackles Rangers' goalkeeper Martin

Sandy Jardine clips the ball into the net for Rangers' second goal after taking on the entire Dunfermline defence

Again – Sandy Jardine, watched by a jubilant Willie Johnstone, shows the determination which has made him such a dangerous striker as he crashes home Rangers' equalizer past Kilmarnock 'keeper Sandy McLaughlan

all her games in Mexico City at the Aztec Stadium where the Final will be played. England did this at Wembley in 1966 and no one could blame Mexico if they followed suit. Here, though, it would give them a tremendous advantage over any other country playing in the finals, because all the acclimatization plans could be knocked for six if a country was to be changing venues constantly, for changing venues means changing altitudes too. This means, of course, some more time to get used to the change in the conditions.

The Mexicans will not be hampered by this. Other teams, especially the hard-running teams such as England, will be.

Don't get me wrong I'm not writing off the English chances of holding on to the Jules Rimet Trophy. I am simply pointing out the difficulties that I realized they would come up against while I was in Mexico.

I still think they will be close, that they will be in at the death, but it will be very, very hard for them to repeat their success.

If any European teams do master the conditions enough to really challenge for the trophy then they could be Yugoslavia and Hungary if they survive the qualifying stages.

Both nations have a style of play that will be more suited to the conditions than England's style. Ball control and technique will play an important part and Yugoslavia have players who combine these talents with a toughness that always makes them formidable opposition. But even more than the Slavs – and I know that they defeated England in the Nations Cup semifinals in Florence last summer – I rate the Hungarians. Hungary has always been able to produce a team of players who can push the ball about intelligently and dangerously. They are the masters at this type of game, a game which slows the pace and which will suit the conditions that teams will face in Mexico. Think back to 1966 and you will remember that the Hungarian team then would have done so much better if they had had a good goalkeeper. That is all that stopped them from being a real threat to England . . .

Still, these are the difficulties. There is one consolation, that no matter what the complaints that can be levelled at the altitude or at the venue selections, no one will be able to complain about the Aztec Stadium itself.

This is a showpiece. I have played all over Europe and America and I cannot remember any stadium that was better than this one. The grass there wasn't too bad either and in most hot countries you don't expect to find that. I understand though that the Mexican authorities are to lay down the artificial grass used in the Astrodome in Houston for the World Cup.

I haven't played on that myself but I have been told by other players that this surface can cause cuts and grazes when you come down on it. I wouldn't imagine that as an improvement.

Anyhow, problems or no problems, I just hope that I will be there with a Scotland team this coming summer. At the moment in the Scottish team we have a tremendous spirit among the lads. We want to get to Mexico. I just hope that it happens.

Because I know that to be there, altitude worries or not, is a wonderful thing. To play in the World Cup Final is to take part in soccer's greatest show on earth. I would like to do it to complete a career in which I've known everything else.

I am a Ball Player

by Jimmy Smith

I AM a ball player, one of the players who have been called the vanishing breed in present-day football.

I suppose that description is fairly accurate because nowadays, the days of defensive football, ball players are scarce and entertainers even scarcer. It isn't like the days when I was a kid growing up in the East End of Glasgow when every Saturday I could watch Celtic and see the greatest entertainers in the game, Charlie Tully and Willie Fernie who were playing for Celtic at that time.

They were the players who influenced me when I was a kid and I suppose even today I still have the urge to play like them as much as possible. I know that my style of play doesn't suit everyone. The fans at Pittodrie haven't been slow to let me know when they are unhappy with the way I am playing but, believe me, I wouldn't change it for anyone or anything.

Being a ball player means that I am in possession of a ball longer than most of my teammates and so the chances of my being caught with a tackle are increased correspondingly. But the way I look at things I reckon if I can

draw a couple of defenders to me by hanging on to the ball then I will be making room for another player. Then, if I can get a pass through to a man lying unmarked I am doing a worthwhile job for the team.

Unfortunately if this type of move fails to come off then I'm left looking silly . . . and the fans are able to see the mistake clearly.

I just don't listen to the crowd on these occasions. All I do is get on with the game and still keep trying to entertain them. That is my main aim because I grew up in that atmosphere built by Tully and Fernie. I was so enthralled by them that I used to go home at night and dream of being a professional footballer.

I did what most Glasgow schoolboys did, played for my school team in the morning then for a juvenile team, Cardown Juveniles it was called, in the afternoon. After that it was the work's team and then Benburb Juniors. That's where Aberdeen saw me play. I'd been with Benburb only six months when the Aberdeen scout in the West of Scotland, Bobby Calder, asked me to sign.

Within a few months I was in the Aberdeen

'I am a ball player, one of the players who have been called the vanishing breed in present-day football.' Jimmy Smith shows how to control the ball

Aberdeen right-back Jimmy Whyte takes a daring header to clear from Bobby Lennox of Celtic. In the end, however, the Dons lost 3–1

first team, playing First Division football. I could hardly believe it was happening to me. That was the kind of thing you used to read about in books, but it doesn't happen so very often in real life.

Because of that chance I will always be grateful to Aberdeen . . . but now I realize the problems of playing with a Scottish provincial team. I don't really think that a player can reach his full potential playing for an unfashionable club. You are ignored a great deal of the time when representative teams are chosen – though I have played in Under-23 games, Inter-League games and one full international against Holland in Amsterdam – and this tends to give you an inferiority complex.

That plus the lack of atmosphere you so often get at the games. I don't think you can ever be

as good as you possibly can be unless you get the opportunity of playing with one of the country's top clubs . . .

That's why I was so disappointed the other year when Aberdeen turned down bids from Liverpool and Celtic for my transfer. I was especially disappointed when Celtic were refused – because they were the team I had followed when I was a youngster. Really, though, the disappointment I felt didn't come because I didn't like Aberdeen as a club. It was simply that I wanted to better myself and this was the only way I could see to do it. I've seen too many good players staying with provincial teams in Scotland and never breaking through into the big time even though they had the talent, to want the same thing to happen to me.

Maybe I wouldn't become all that much

113

Going for the ball in an Aberdeen v. Celtic match last January better as a player, but I think I owe it to myself to try.

It's just a sad fact of soccer life that clubs such as Aberdeen cannot compete with either Celtic or Rangers economically. It has given the competition in Scotland a badly-balanced look and nothing except drastic League reconstruction can ever change it.

There is one important lesson I think I have now learned at Pittodrie, one that should help me in the future, that is how to control my temper.

I was twice in trouble with the Referee Committee and I suppose it was because of my style of play. Ball players are more subject to hard tackling than other players.

Several times I couldn't stand the hard tackling and I retaliated. Now I have made a determined effort to stop hitting back. I wasn't helping anyone behaving that way. My own game was suffering and if I was suspended then my team was suffering too. It was silly and the only way to beat the problem was to discipline myself. I've been reasonably successful in staying clear of trouble and it's a lesson that I think everyone has to learn some time. A lot of things in football aren't easy to accept but you have to learn to accept the bad with the good . . . otherwise you will never be a really great player.

When I think of a top player I think of Bobby Charlton – and I remember his tremendous behaviour on the field under all kinds of provocation. He is an outstanding example to every player.

After playing against him in the Scottish League v. English League game last season I'm even more convinced of that.

My early idols were the Parkhead entertainers Charlie Tully and Willie Fernie. One of my new idols is Bobby Charlton, the gentleman of Old Trafford.

'When I think of a top player I think of Bobby Charlton' – here seen cutting between two Scots in an England v. Scotland international at Wembley

Sportswriter

by Ken Gallacher

THE schoolboy's dream – if it isn't becoming a football player – is probably to have the kind of job that I have. A sportswriter whose main job is reporting on the big Scottish football games for my newspaper, the Scottish *Daily Record*.

It's a job that has taken me to most of the countries in Europe and across the Atlantic to the United States and Canada. I have seen scores of top games in all these countries following the Scottish international team and our leading club teams, Celtic, Rangers, Dunfermline, Dundee and Dundee United.

The games and the exciting places they have been played provide a touch of romance to the job . . . when you're looking from the sidelines. For just as in everything else the job has its problems. Problems that seem funny when you can look back on them after a few years but which, at the time, seemed the end of the world . . .

Like the time I was covering a game in the little town of Hamilton, Ontario where Celtic on their tour of Canada and the United States were playing the local team Hamilton Primos. It was one of three or four games where Celtic were playing local opposition and they were piling up a few goals. In ordinary circumstances it was an easy game to report . . . but not that summer's night!

For the first problem we had the time difference between Canada and Glasgow, five hours which meant the game would not finish until around 2 a.m. back home, a very late finish for our edition.

Still, the telephones had been good until then so I felt fairly confident. Then came the day of the game. A quick reconnaissance found there were no phones in the Press box. Downstairs below the stand there were half a dozen call boxes, but only one of them was working. I decided this would have to do the job. A trans-Atlantic call from a phone box may sound awkward but in the States it isn't too bad . . . unless something goes wrong as it did in Hamilton.

The first-half message was all right. I phoned from the box at half-time without any trouble.

Then came the call near the end of the game and when I rushed downstairs I discovered a teen-ager inside the only box calling his girl friend. I was forced to wait around outside for several minutes then with the thought of the edition time looming up I eventually interrupted him and explained. He looked at me as if I were some kind of nut before finally agreeing to come off the line. I made the edition by ten minutes . . .

I wasn't so lucky once before when I was in Lisbon covering a European Cup game involving Dundee and Sporting Club of Portugal. The day before the game I had arranged for the office to call me at my hotel just after lunch-time. So, from midday onwards I sat in my room waiting for the phone to ring. I had lunch in the room, dinner in the room and eventually the call came at midnight . . . too late for the Dundee edition.

For almost five years that remained my memory of Lisbon and it was only wiped out by the European Cup Final when Celtic beat Inter Milan. That was the night that Lisbon belonged to the Celtic supporters who thronged the pavement cafés to sing their songs of victory . . .

Newspapermen have different ways of look-ing at countries. As a rule we don't really like heading for Spain or Portugal because com-munications can be so difficult. It's no joke when you find yourself sitting in the stand reporting a vital game and the phone goes dead in your hand. That has happened so often to so many of us.

Then, also, it isn't too nice to head behind the Iron Curtain for the same reasons. Once, with Celtic again, on a European Cup Winners Cup trip to Tbilisi in the south of Russia, the only thing that saved us was that we had a two hours time difference in our favour.

I'll always remember that trip, too, because of the way Celtic trainer Neil Mochan handed out hunks of cheese to the Press who had been living on ice-cream, the one thing which was completely edible in our hotel. And the best after-match banquet I've had, cheese and crackers in John Hughes' room after the game . . . the first food I'd been able to eat all day.

Then, of course, there was the time the boot was on the other foot, and, again behind the Iron Curtain. This time it was with Rangers and we were travelling to Dresden for a Fairs Cities Cup game. The Press were told to travel with the team by coach from Berlin Airport, so we set out with the players, all of us, by this time, tired and hungry after the journey. With-in seven or eight miles of starting out from the airport there was a sound of sirens and a police motor cyclist waved us down. We wondered what was wrong. Was there a visa not in order? Were we going to have to turn back?

It turned out to be much simpler than that. On to the bus came a government courier with packed meals . . . but only for the Pressmen! So that time it was our turn to look after the players . . .

These are some of the off-field stories. But the real drama is on the field and watching Dundee United, European unknowns, shocking Barcelona at their own magnificent Stadium, or Celtic beating Inter Milan in Lisbon, or Rangers holding out with ten men against Borussia Dortmund, or watching goalkeeper Jim Herriot, now with Birmingham, but then with Dunfermline, saving a last-minute penalty in Stuttgart to stop his team from going out of the Fairs Cities Cup. These are the other great memories, memories that no newspaperman would ever forget.

The memories that make the job so worth-while.

Schoolboy Rangers: Opportunities Today

by John Greig

IBROX is now invaded during every school holiday by the newest Rangers' recruits . . . every one of them a schoolboy!

This is the new system started by the club last year, a system where they hope to unearth new young stars for the team. And, believe me, it's a system that I wish the Scottish clubs had used when I was a youngster. I didn't have the same chance as these lads are getting now, nor did any of the players who are the same age as myself.

Because, at that time, Scottish clubs could not sign players who were still at school. Now the rules have been changed and Rangers even signed a thirteen-year-old boy from Broxburn Academy last year.

The advantages that these boys have are tremendous. When I first went to Ibrox I was seventeen, a provisional signing who trained with the part-time players and really picked up information about the game only from listening to the older lads and from my own experience in the practice games we had.

Now all that has altered. For the first big football teach-in that the club organized the Scottish Football Association coach Roy Small, the man who bosses Scotland's professional youth team, took charge.

The boys weren't coming to train away and kick a ball about – they were coming to learn about the tactics and the more sophisticated techniques of the game.

They were being shown how to play three men against two, how to use the wall pass, how best to make advantage from having an extra man in certain situations. They learned about the different formations and why they were used.

It was a complete run-down on the technical side of the game which is so often ignored by teachers at school. At school the boys are encouraged to develop their own natural skills . . . but sometimes that isn't enough. These youngsters are maturing faster now, and therefore they have to learn the more advanced stages of the game.

I feel pretty strongly about this. I think, for instance, that professional footballers should get the opportunity to coach these kids while they are at school. I know that players do this

117

down South and I think that helps in the development of the game there. I know that if it were possible I'd gladly give up time to coach

When I was a youngster the only clubs who specialized in coaching of this kind were the top teams in England. We used to be told that we

Dave White, manager of Rangers, with some of the youngsters at a football teach-in

schoolboys, to give them the benefit of my experience.

Still, in a way, the new set-up that Rangers are using helps to do this. These young boys are going to be able to learn far more about the game at an earlier age than I could.

should play for Manchester United or Everton and get the benefits of top-class coaching that we would never get in Scotland.

I'm happy to say that that old idea is changing. It's out of date now the way that Rangers and Celtic and some of the other clubs are dis-

Crowded goalmouth scene in the match between East Stirling and St Johnstone

I want to ring bells! Dundee United players in happy mood after scoring against Ayr United in the Cup

covering young talent and working hard with the schoolboy stars.

I take a look around at the young players today and there's Tommy Craig of Aberdeen, still eligible for the youth team but a regular First Division player who has played in two European games. And at Ibrox we have young Alfie Conn, the son of the former Hearts' inside man, who is another player who has played in a Fairs Cities Cup game while he's still only sixteen. Our manager, David White, decided that Alfie needed this experience and on he came in the second half of our game against the Irish club Dundalk in Ireland.

This is the type of thing which is becoming the usual practice . . . instead of being the exception it was when I was trying to break through into the Rangers' team.

Eventually I think the whole of Scotland will benefit from this type of coaching going to youngsters. You take a look at so many England international teams and you find that players – Bobby Moore is the best example – have come up from the youth team, through the Under-23's and into the full team. That is why I see great hope for the future of Scottish international football. The players I have mentioned, Tommy Craig and Alfie Conn, plus several others are coming through the youth team internationals and learning all the time.

And, at the club level, where I can only talk really about Rangers, I see these youngsters becoming a part of the club.

When they came to the stadium for their first spell of training you could see that most of them were a bit over-awed by everything. After all, they were coming straight from school and working out alongside international players . . . it all seemed a little too much. Then the Boss and the assistant manager, Willie Thornton, introduced them to the first-team lads and the shyness soon left them.

Now I think they are beginning to feel part of the club because they are guests at any of the games they can manage to get along to. If they aren't playing themselves they come along to Ibrox and all the time they are getting closer to the spirit of the club.

And when they have matured physically they will take less time to break through to first-team standard than I did or anyone else from my age group. They are learning things now that took us many seasons to grasp . . .

That's why the scheme will pay off for the club and for the country. For a generation of players with tactical knowledge allied to the basic skills is coming . . . and everyone is going to benefit.

We hope you have enjoyed this book.
You are cordially invited to write for full details of our Sports Books.